ENGLISH PAINTERS
HOGARTH TO CONSTABLE

These lectures were delivered as part of a Community Art Program sponsored by The Carnegie Corporation of New York.

ANDREW C. RITCHIE

ENGLISH PAINTERS

HOGARTH TO CONSTABLE

LECTURES DELIVERED APRIL 9, 10, 11, 16, 17, 1940
AT THE JOHNS HOPKINS UNIVERSITY

Essay Index Reprint Series

BOOKS FOR LIBRARIES PRESS
FREEPORT, NEW YORK

LIBRARY OF CONGRESS CATALOG CARD NUMBER:

68-57337

CONTENTS

LIST OF PLATES

INTRODUCTION

I must first of all express my gratitude to the Curriculum in Fine Arts of the Johns Hopkins University for making possible the original presentation of these lectures and now their publication in book form. For their kind permission to reproduce their pictures, I am also deeply grateful to the many private and public owners whose courtesy is specifically acknowledged on the plates in question. I am deeply indebted to Miss Helen Franc of the Pierpont Morgan Library for reading my manuscript.

England's contribution to painting since the Renaissance has usually been considered a minor one. The English as a nation have been accused of having stunted sensibilities so far as the visual arts are concerned. One of their own great critics, Roger Fry, has even charged them with what amounts to a congenital optical deficiency. According to this indictment the Englishman lacks depth perception, and consequently all his visual images are flat. This limited, two-dimensional view, Fry would have held, explains the English genius for line drawing, so splendidly exemplified in illuminated manuscripts; but faced with the sculptural three-dimensional requirements of post-medieval, Italian-derived, painting the Englishman found himself at a huge disadvantage.

Now while such a charge may contain an element of truth (along with much exaggeration) my position in these lectures is not a defensive one. There is much to be said on the credit side of English painting. In making our estimate, however, we must look beyond the fashionable Society portrait, the sentiment for which has noticeably cooled in recent years. If we do so I think we shall see that England's contribution to painting in the 18th and early 19th centuries has a certain significance for later art both in and out of England.

English 18th century painting was produced under more modern conditions, on the whole, than those with which, for example, contemporary French art had to contend. At this time England in certain respects was ahead of France—and all other countries of Europe for that matter. That her advanced political, social, and economic position was reflected in the kind and quality of her artistic expression is, therefore, not surprising.

I am here referring not so much to technical accomplishments in painting, as such, but rather to total artistic trends. We cannot say, for example, that Hogarth is a greater painter, as painter, than Boucher; that Gainsborough outstripped Fragonard. What we must appreciate is that Hogarth, Gainsborough, and their fellows were faced with a set of social and economic conditions which were essentially more forward-looking in character than any to be found elsewhere in Europe.

In this connection one distinguishing characteristic of the English 18th century painter should be stressed. He found it necessary in a number of instances to write on art as well as to paint. And as a consequence, of course, his paintings cannot be completely understood without some knowledge of his writings. But the very fact that Hogarth, Reynolds, and Blake—to name only three—felt called upon to write at all seems to me a significant modern phenomenon, in that they wrote partly in defense of their own practice as artists and partly in order to educate a backward or unwilling English patron in the criticism and appreciation of their painting. The hiatus that has existed in modern times, then, between the taste of the painter and the taste of the public would seem to have been first established and recognized in 18th century England.

Before the 18th century an outstanding European artist rarely expressed himself on matters of art through the printed word. There was seldom any necessity for him do so, at least by way of defense, since it was the rule for artists either to follow the tastes of their patrons, more or less, or for patrons to follow theirs. (Vasari and Pacheco were primarily historians of painting, and they were not particularly significant painters in their own right.) Hogarth's and Blake's resort to writing, on the other hand, grew out of sheer necessity: they were acutely conscious of a serious gap existing between their artistic intentions and the appreciation or understanding of those intentions by their English public. Their experience in this regard was not unusual; it was the rule rather than the exception for the artist of their time in England to find his most original efforts rejected or discountenanced. Richard Wilson, the first great English landscape painter, died in abject poverty—the direct result of public neglect. James Barry, follower and protégé of Reynolds, took his own life, an act which was in part due to public misunderstanding or lack of appreciation of his work. Reynolds, sensitive as he was to public taste, found it expedient to prepare the ground for the reception of his pictures by his *Discourses*. Gainsborough suffered frustration of half his genius by his public's refusal to buy his landscapes. Blake's public generally considered him somewhat mad, although the causes there are not so hard to understand—his extremely personal expression would probably have met difficulties of appreciation in almost any age before our own. Constable had to wait until the last decade of his life for any public acclaim, and even then it was given somewhat grudgingly. And so the story goes. While not all of these painters wrote, when one did find himself articulate in a literary way is it any wonder that he took up the pen?

This phenomenon of the English artist-writer, and the divorce which it so often implies between artist and public (a divorce not present in France at the same time, be it noted; hence no 18th century French artist felt called upon to write) is nothing more than a reflection, however, of the leading characteristics of many English 18th century artists—their insistence upon painting sometimes as they pleased. They did not always paint as they pleased, to be sure, and they did not always paint well, but surely it is because of their more than occasionally individualistic outlook that the school which they represent shows such an extraordinary diversity of talents and personalities—again a modern phenomenon.

By contrast, French artists like Watteau, Boucher, and Fragonard were less independent, less overtly individualistic because they identified themselves more closely with the interests of their patrons. They were, in fact, artist-servants and their art was consequently never far removed from the taste of their masters. Furthermore, they were docile members of a society which on the surface was stable in manners, customs, and institutions, no matter how pregnant these were with change. There was little place under such a regime for the kind of individualistic painting which Hogarth and others in England were forced or permitted to produce.

England had had her revolution in 1688 and from that time on the rise to power of a rich merchant society is the most significant single factor in changing the political, economic, and social face of the country. The old landed aristocrats of Stuart times, comparable in their status and the sources of their wealth and power to French 18th century society, were forced more and more into the background. The stresses set up by this friction between the old Tories and the new merchant Whigs produced a dynamic, even violent, social atmosphere. And just as the Whig demand for individual liberty of action was to have its most splendid flowering in 19th century democratic liberalism, so, too the fervent individualism of painters like Hogarth, Blake, and Constable foreshadows the determined independence of a Cézanne or a Picasso.

New York, April 1940.

CHAPTER I

WILLIAM HOGARTH

The social forces which helped to shape the outlook of a Hogarth gave rise, as is well known, to a growing literature of social commentary and criticism. Addison's and Steele's *Spectator* in the early years of the 18th century gives the first important indication of what is to follow in the development of popular opinion on matters of every sort. By means of the press, from single sheet broadsides to newspapers and magazines, a popular instrument of communication was formed. From this awakened interest in the news, and the growth of a reading public which it implied, came the beginnings of the novel under Richardson and Fielding. The essay, the newspaper, the novel, and the increasingly popular play are all of great importance for an understanding of the period—and particularly for an understanding of Hogarth. For Hogarth, aside from his other qualities as an artist, attempted to reflect, pictorially, something of the variety, richness, and violence of Georgian life, so splendidly recorded by the literary men of the age. If only as a great illustrator—and he was much more—he is one of the most varied and certainly one of the most vital figures in the history of English painting.

Born in 1697, he lived until 1764. In the main his painting preceded all but the earliest work of Reynolds and Gainsborough. He literally dominates the English painting scene of the first half of the century, for, numerous though his contemporaries were—Highmore, Richardson, Hudson, and the rest—they come off on the whole only a poor second best beside him. Nevertheless, if he is the most important artist of his time, he is also the most uneven. He attempted almost every form of painting, with the possible exception of landscape; but, great though his technical ability was, his chief material success was derived not from paintings themselves but from the prints he engraved and had engraved after them.

As portrait painter he found early in life that he was unable to command a sufficient income, as he tells us himself. Probably because of his belligerent independence of spirit he was unable to play the necessary game of social flattery which, to some extent, has always been demanded of the professional portrait painter. This inability to adjust himself to the mood of certain of his sitters, with whom he otherwise felt no sympathy, must have precluded much insight into any subtleties of their characters. As a result, although the number of portraits Hogarth painted throughout a fairly long life is a large one, only a few are particularly distinguished in conception or design, and still fewer are marked by any great psychological penetration. Those few, however, are marked, when he pleases, with a brilliant directness of observation.

His deservedly most famous is that of *Captain Coram* (Plate 1 a), in the Foundling Hospital, London, founder and genial benefactor of that famous institution. With what appears to be a good mixture of business acumen and humanitarian sympathy for the foundling project, Hogarth presented the governors of the hospital with the portrait in 1740. Other artists followed suit, among them Richard Wilson, Highmore, Hayman, and Gainsborough, and the hospital in effect became the first public exhibition place in London for paintings. This portrait explains at once Hogarth's failure to please the fashionable portrait patron of his day. It is a curious combination of baroque portrait " business " and a direct realistic portrayal of the shrewd little cockney captain. The column and curtain are, of course, traditional Italianate portrait properties. In the Van Dyck formula, from which Hogarth's picture eventually derives, these properties are intended to give an added sense of elongation and hence elevated stature to the sitter further to emphasize his superior social status. *Captain Coram* is hardly a successful essay in this form of genteel design. He is obviously a small man. His legs barely reach the floor; but actually he appears smaller, in contrast to the weighty vertical accents of his background. What saves the picture from the ridiculous is the downright honesty and masterful directness of treatment of the captain himself. Goya has not painted anything more psychologically dynamic than this.

There is less directness of treatment, although a greater economy of design, in the portrait of *Frederick Frankland* (Plate 1 b), in the Huntington Library and Art Gallery, California. Despite the convincing handling of the figure, there is a somewhat insensitive rendering of the face, producing a wooden-like characterization. This mask which Hogarth substitutes at times for a living delineation of features, where he lacks sufficient interest in, or sympathy for, the sitter, can verge on what must be unintentional caricature—for example, his portrait of *William James* (Plate 2 a), in the Worcester (Massachusetts) Art Museum. On the other hand, when he can throw aside the conventional inhibitions of the professional portrait painter and paint exactly what he sees, he can produce the well-known *Shrimp Girl,* in the Tate Gallery, London—a marvel of fluent impressionistic technique rivaling the work of Hals.

Unfortunately, this type of unconventional portrait—if the *Shrimp Girl* is a portrait at all in the accepted sense of the word— is the exception in Hogarth's general practice. There are only a few others which are free from the taint of a conventional pose or a mask-like expression. Two of these are certainly the first examples of sensational pictorial journalism—now so adequately handled by our tabloid press. One is the portrait of the murderess *Sarah Malcolm* (Plate 2 b), painted from life in the condemned cell of Newgate prison in 1733. That she was a Catholic (her rosary is on the table before her) undoubtedly added to her guilt, given Hogarth's and his public's anti-Catholic prejudice. She looks, however, singularly unrepentant (she had murdered three people in a robbery), or at least the artist has chosen so to represent her. He is characteristically unsentimental in his treatment of her predicament. His Low Church morality is too severe to permit sympathy in such a case. He may hate cruelty to man or beast on humanitarian grounds, but for a crime or a sin the punishment with him must always fit the deed.

[3]

Even more interesting, in a journalistic sense, is his brilliantly drawn portrait of *Simon Fraser, Lord Lovat* (Plate 3 a), a Scottish rebel during the 1745 Highland uprising. Lovat was arrested and brought to London in 1746 to stand trial for treason and was later executed. So determined was Hogarth to get a journalistic " scoop " on this notorious character, he journeyed to St. Albans, twelve miles outside London, to see him before he was brought to the capital. Since both the *Sarah Malcolm* and the *Lovat* portraits were designed for translation into prints for popular sale, Hogarth had to be a sharp reporter and, if possible, get to the criminal in both instances before his competitors.

The directness of approach in these uncommissioned portraits (the *Group Portrait of His Servants* is another famous example) is to be found in a few of Hogarth's great canvases outside portraiture. Notable among these is *The Dance* (Plate 3 b), in the South London Art Gallery. As an engraving it was used as one of the principal explanatory illustrations in the artist's *Analysis of Beauty*. His comment on the plate, as Austin Dobson has said,[1] " anticipates some of the revelations of modern instantaneous photography." It reads:

The best representation in a picture, of even the most elegant dancing, as every figure is rather suspended action in it than an attitude, must always be somewhat unnatural and ridiculous: for were it possible in a real dance to fix every person at one instant of time, as in a picture, not one in twenty would appear to be graceful, tho' each were ever so much so in their movements; nor could the figure of the dance itself be at all understood.[2]

Surely no artist before Degas has made such an acute observation with reference to the drawing of movement, and the latter's marvelous eye and recording hand were certainly aided by the study of photographs.

The " modernity " of *The Dance* and the uncommissioned portraits brings us to another phase of Hogarth's art. It is always well to remember that he did not begin his artistic career in the

[1] *William Hogarth* (New York: The McClure Co., 1907), p. 114.
[2] *Analysis of Beauty* (London, 1753), p. 137.

way usual to most English artists in the 18th century—painting portraits. He was first apprenticed to a silver engraver and quickly turned from decorative silver designs to engravings for book illustrations and the like. He begins, then, with the graving tool, working in black and white, and comes to painting in oils as a secondary, though finally, for him, most important medium of expression. But his engraver's training—the reproduction of another artist's compositions—undoubtedly shaped his painting career, at least in his choice of subject matter. In fact, perhaps only with this training was it possible for him to break away from the bondage of portraiture, aginst which many an English artist struggled in vain.

His early book illustrations, such as those for Butler's *Hudibras* done in the 1720's, demanded a sense of dramatic values in the depiction of action and the grouping of characters in a scene. It is not surprising, then, that he early turns to a new type of picture in English art which he considered, whether rightly or wrongly, an invention of his, the so-called conversation piece. A good example is *A Family Group* (Plate 4 a), in the National Gallery, London. It represents a distinctively informal treatment of the everyday life of the gentry of Hogarth's time. It has a pleasantly intimate air of casualness as a picture type, and in this sense it is truly English, although its diverse roots are certainly in the Dutch family portrait and the French *fêtes galantes*. Other examples of the type are *The Family Portrait* and *The Fontaine Family* in the Pennsylvania Museum of Art, Philadelphia, *Three Figures in a Room* in The Pierpont Morgan Library, New York (a good example of Hogarth's wash drawing technique) and *Daniel Woodbridge and Captain Holland Drinking Wine,* in the Marshall Field collection, New York.

During this same period of the late 1720's and early 1730's Hogarth painted a number of group portraits related in some ways to the conversation piece but lacking its intimacy of sentiment and domestic casualness of grouping. There is one particularly which should be seen alongside the portraits of Sarah Malcolm and Lovat: *A Committee of the House of Commons examining*

Bambridge, a brutally corrupt jailor of Fleet Street Prison (Plate 4 b). It has all their journalistic timeliness; but, it must be said, it shows more concern apparently for the documentation of an actual scene than for any compositional artistry. The same is true of two much more genteel documents, *The Assembly at Wanstead House,* in the Pennsylvania Museum of Art, Philadelphia, and *The Wedding of Stephen Beckingham and Mary Cox* (Plate 5 a), in the Metropolitan Museum of Art, New York. The awkward horizontal lineup of heads in both these pictures, their lack of any subtlety in design, in other words, is an indication of a major weakness in composition which Hogarth at his best never quite succeeds in correcting. The truth is he was not sufficiently concerned with composition as such to give it the attention it deserved. His controlling interest was content and its dramatic, moral, or satirical significance. What he never seems to have fully recognized was that the effectiveness of his " story " was closely dependent upon the clarity and economy of his presentation.

The dramatic overtones in his conversation pieces and documentary pictures are a direct product of Hogarth's interest, in the late 1720's, in the theater. He saw in stage performances the possibility of a new kind of picture which would help to break down his public's preoccupation with the portrait. Of this period of his career he writes:

[Portrait painting was] not sufficiently profitable to pay the expenses my family required. I therefore turned my thoughts to a still more novel mode, *viz.,* painting and engraving modern moral subjects, a field not broken up in any country or any age. . . . I . . . wished to compose pictures on canvas, similar to representations on the stage; and farther hope, that they will be tried by the same test, and criticised by the same criterion. Let it be observed that I mean to speak only of those scenes where the human species are actors, and these I think have not often been delineated in a way of which they are worthy and capable. In these compositions, those subjects that will both entertain and improve the mind, bid fair to be of the greatest public utility, and must therefore be entitled to rank in the highest class . . . I have endeavoured to treat my subject as a dramatic writer; my picture is my stage, and men and women my players, who by

means of certain actions and gestures, are to exhibit a *dumb show*. . . .
This I found was most likely to answer my purpose, provided I could
strike the passions and by small sums from many, by the sale of prints
which I could engrave from my own pictures, thus secure my property
to myself.[3]

As a sort of preliminary training for this pictorial moral theater,
it would appear, Hogarth illustrated at least two scenes from
actual plays. His *Scene from Gay's " Beggar's Opera,"* painted
1728-29, in the Tate Gallery, London, is one of these (Plate 5 b).
Here he chose to depict the popular, because " pathetic," Newgate
prison scene, where the two mistresses of the hero Macheath, Lucy
Lockit and Polly Peachum, beseech their respective fathers, the
jailor (on the left) and the highwayman's fence (on the right)
for the release of the manacled prisoner. As is well known, the
Beggars' Opera was a satire on the sentimental morality of contemporary plays. The sad result of Jeremy Collier's criticism and
Richard Steele's example, these were written, ostensibly, to correct
the looseness of morals which had marked the Restoration drama,
by a sentimental appeal to the moral righteousness of the audience.
Hogarth's choice of a play to depict is, therefore, significant.
Choosing a comic satire he comes down on the unsentimental side,
and throughout his career, it will be noted, his downright, Low
Church, cockney sense of right and wrong seldom gives way to
maudlin pity for virtue lost or honor destroyed.

The second stage scene (Plate 6 a), painted in 1731, and now
in Lord Ilchester's collection, London, is interesting because of
its child actors. The play, however, a private performance of
Dryden's heroic tragedy *The Indian Emperor,* is much the strangest
vehicle ever to be used by juvenile performers. It is more than
curious also that from such unrelated dramas as Gay's comic opera
and Dryden's tragedy, Hogarth perhaps with a libertarian sympathy has chosen for representation scenes in which the hero is in
manacles or chains. The composition of both these scenes is of
interest in the light of the remarks made above on this feature of
Hogarth's work; in both there is an unusual attention given to the

[3] John Ireland, *Hogarth Illustrated,* vol. III, pp. 26-28, 29, 31. (Quoted by
Dobson, *op. cit.,* pp. 33-34.)

value of strong diagonal accents to suggest movement and to tie the compositions together. How can we explain this relatively expert compositional treatment? Surely it is because Hogarth is here assisted by a pre-arranged setting and disposition of figures on the stage. Where he had to fall back on his own invention, however, for assembling a group of figures, his weakness in this respect reveals itself once more. Following his own preoccupation his imagination was impressed once again by the subject of the dramatic scene. The stage presentation he might record more or less faithfully, but its compositional influence on him was only secondary.

We must now turn to the mature phase of Hogarth's career, the period from the early 1730's until his death in 1764. During that time he was chiefly concerned with staging and marketing his own moral and satirical plays in prints, for which as we have seen he had been steadily preparing himself. Since the second half of the 18th century until today there has been a steady stream of commentary and criticism on him as a moralist. First the " meaning " of his prints was repeatedly exposed in almost fatuous detail —a practice continuing well into the 19th century. The Victorians above all, through their strong penchant for anecdote, and particularly sentimental moral anecdote, raised his reputation in this respect to a great height, at the expense of many other qualities in his work. It was not until the turn of the present century, when the progress of reaction to Victorian literary standards of art criticism made itself felt, that Hogarth began to receive part of his due as an artist pure and simple.

The judgments of both the traditional and modern schools of appreciation have been in many ways mutually exclusive; those primarily interested in understanding or expounding (and to do one was to attempt the other) the moral meaning of his prints valued him hardly at all as a painter; or rather they chose to think that in the variety and fervor of his moral " tracts " lay his great work as an artist. On the other hand, the critics of more recent years, in trying to redress the balance, have chosen to see in Hogarth a painter of potentially the first rank in Europe whose production was almost ruined by his over-anxiety to point a moral in almost everything he did. This dual nature of Hogarth's reputation, moralist on the one hand, painter on the other, may appear at first to be due simply to a change of taste. We are inclined to think that future consideration will discover, however, that the explanation is to be found in part in the makeup of the artist himself.

It is significant, first of all, that even in his own day Hogarth's reputation in certain circles depended on a "literary" rather than a pictorial evaluation of his work. Fielding's well-known comment is worth recalling in this connection. In the introduction to *Joseph Andrews*, speaking of Hogarth, he says:

It hath been thought a vast Commendation of a Painter, to say his figures "seem to breathe," but surely [and he seems to be criticizing here those connoisseurs who sought to underrate Hogarth as a painter] it is a much greater and nobler Applause, "that they appear to think."

Such an estimate was only possible from one who "read" a Hogarth print or canvas rather than one who enjoyed it and was moved by it first of all as a picture.

Surely Hogarth is primarily responsible for this division of interest in his work. His writings indicate, as we have seen, that he wanted his pictures to be judged on dramatic standards, not painterly ones. Having taken this line, he was too often, although not always, the moralist first, forcing his painting for this purpose into a subsidiary role. (It is well to remember too, of course, that for the thousands who saw his prints, only a handful saw the original paintings from which they had been taken.) He imagined a scene or situation in its moral rather than its visual aspect, and the result tended to be a canvas or print packed to the edges with every conceivable detail which might ram home his criticism. Take, for example, the two famous prints *Gin Lane* and *Beer Street* (Plates 6 b, 6 c), designed as a moral on the evil effects attendant upon the over consumption of cheap gin by the masses towards the middle of the 18th century in London, as opposed to the beneficent and healthful influence of good English beer. It will be noted what an amazing naïveté underlies Ho-

[9]

garth's moral lesson. If you drink gin, he says, evil will follow; if you drink beer, good will result. It is perhaps characteristic of all moralities that they depend for their effect, if not their validity, on such black and white contrasts. However that may be, to Hogarth's non-latitudinarian, Low Church outlook, right is always right and wrong wrong, and there can be no shades of truth between. This positive attitude marks all his lessons, whether he is depicting *A Harlot's Progress* (1731), *A Rake's Progress* (1735), or the course of a marriage of convenience in *Marriage à la Mode* (1745). In each series the end is always disaster (not tragedy in the Aristotelian sense, it will be noted, because there are no alternative lines of action for the protagonists in his dramas). To him nothing is more sure than the biblical adage " The wages of sin is death." His harlot comes to a speedy end; his rake goes mad; and the young couple in *Marriage à la Mode* die violently, he in a duel, she by poison.

So far we have spoken of Hogarth chiefly as a moralist rather than a satirist, although both terms have been applied to him indiscriminately. There is some confusion here, and again Hogarth himself is responsible. The moralist strictly speaking has always felt called upon to depict evil in an ugly or loathsome light in order that by inducing a state of revulsion in the onlooker he will drive him to what he considers the good life. But while Hogarth by no means prettifies any of the steps in *Marriage à la Mode,* he is not content with what might be called simple loathsomeness in his representation; he also ridicules. For example in " The Contract " (Plate 7 a) scene the titled lord, full of gout and pointing to his family tree, is a figure of fun, as is the detail of the two dogs chained to each other symbolizing the bored young couple; and likewise in " The Toilet Scene " (Plate 7 b) the predominant note throughout is one of ridicule of affected manners —rather than repulsiveness. Now if the loathsomeness of evil is a preachment of the moralist, ridicule is the weapon of the satirist. So that here as elsewhere Hogarth uses two sticks to beat the dog. The result often proves that the animal was dead before he started—in other words, the moral attack tends to neutralize the satirical attack, and vice versa.

And here is one of the chief criticisms of Hogarth as an artist. The motivating roots of a moral art and a satirical art are radically different, although their intentions may be similar or identical—to lay bare or destroy the object or action under criticism. In a word, moral criticism is never individual criticism alone; the resentment of the thing abhorred is born of a social or religious convention or dogma, and the individual artist is simply an instrument of expression. Satire, on the other hand, is a personal not a communal matter; it is born usually in periods of social dislocation or change, such as was true of Hogarth's time, when the artist tends to be thrown back on himself as an instrument of judgment, and his anger or hate, by a violent process of sublimation, is expressed in a ridiculing or caricaturing of the object under criticism. In many of Hogarth's prints, however, the sources of his distaste are confused. Compared, say, with the bitter effectiveness of Goya's satires on war, or the moral persuasiveness of a medieval Last Judgment, his preachments all too often miss fire. Many of his pictures are no more than amusing catalogues of the objects and people of his time. When such a print is neither strictly moral nor satirical, but a mixture of both, one begins to feel unconsciously a lack of sincerity in it. The artist shouts too much, gesticulates too easily, to be perhaps altogether convincing.

Fortunately he was not always so confused. In a number of individual paintings and in at least one late series, *Four Prints of an Election,* where the point of his criticism is purely satirical, the force and vitality of his expression is unquestioned. There is force too, and singleness of critical purpose, in the *Sleeping Congregation,* a satire on the dull preaching of the times in the established church—a dullness which finally produced a Methodist revolution. *The Gate of Calais,* in the National Gallery, London, an anti-papist and anti-jacobite broadside, is also simon-pure satire. And finally consider the wit of *Taste in High Life* (Plate 8 a), a picture painted for Miss Mary Edwards, a lady who possessed one of the greatest fortunes in England. Her independent eccentricities of behaviour, and particularly her unconventional style in dresses, were the subject of much amused criticism in London high society. As an answer to such criticism she asked Hogarth to paint a picture which would point the finger of scorn at her critics, and it is clear that he did not fail her. He also did a portrait of her which is now in the Frick Collection, New York (Plate 8 b). Among many of her foibles was, it seems, a marked distaste for husbands who run off with their wives' money. Her own husband, an indigent nobleman, Lord Ann Hamilton, she found guilty of such an offense and quite on her own, so the story goes, without benefit of the law, declared her marriage null and void, and tore up the marriage papers. Hogarth's vindication of her, and her action, and, it might well be, a vindication of his own rebellious, independent temper is contained in a sort of ode to liberty which is inscribed on the scroll to the lady's right:

> Remember Englishmen the Laws the Rights
> The Generous plan of Power deliver'd down
> From age to age by your renown'd Forefathers
> So Dearly bought the Price of so much contest
> Transmit it careful to Posterity
> Do thou great Liberty inspire their Souls
> And make their Lives in thy possession happy
> Or their Deaths Glorious in thy Just defence.

On this note of liberty of action we may conclude. Despite his occasional confusion of moral and satirical criticism, a confusion which is part and parcel of his irrational belligerent nature, that Hogarth was at times a great satirist and very often a painter of great accomplishment there can be no doubt. Within the limitations of one chapter it has not been possible to discuss anything like a fully representative body of his paintings. But in those few works which have been mentioned the reader will perhaps have seen enough to agree that he is one of the most vital, original, various, and individual geniuses that England has produced.

CHAPTER II

SIR JOSHUA REYNOLDS

In contrast to Hogarth's independent, contemporary outlook Reynolds is a distinctly reactionary figure. Perhaps for that reason his life and his art contain little that is spectacular. His production and reputation have a ponderous, premeditated quality which smacks a little of the Bank of England. Like it he has become an English institution, and like it also his façade is more weighty than ornamental. It is not by chance that he has been called the Samuel Johnson of English painting. Johnson was his friend and not only helped him touch up his famous *Discourses* but, as Reynolds tells us, he did much to shape his mind.

Like Johnson, though lacking his thunder, he represents in his art theories a conservative worship of tradition which is paralleled politically in England by the return of the Tory party to power in the last quarter of the 18th century. The liberty of the individual which Hogarth lauded in his portrait of *Miss Mary Edwards* was successfully checked and did not come to life again until the period of parliamentary reform in the 1830's. The Whigs under Walpole had steadily broken the power of George I and II, who could hardly speak English, and centered authority more and more in Parliament. The Tories, under Lord North, came to power in 1770 and to reverse this trend were popularly called "King's men" for their support of George III. While Reynolds, with clients of all persuasions, had to remain more or less politically neutral, his dedicatory remarks to the King in his first *Discourse*, delivered in his capacity as first President at the opening of the Royal Academy in 1769, may show the new trend. They appear to be more than a mere formality and pay genuine homage to royalty for its support of the Academy project. In fact, like the United States, had it not been for George III, the Academy might never have been.

[13]

With such traditional authority behind the Academy, it is not surprising that Reynolds throughout his career sought to emulate some of the great artists of the past. The past to him was golden. The great age of painting was over but by diligent study, he felt, it was possible to recover some of the glory that was Italy. The worshipful inferiority which such an attitude implies, given Reynolds' tremendous influence as artist and as theorist, did much to undermine the vitality of the English school—so recently come to life under Hogarth.

Before Reynolds, English painting had drawn sustenance from the sensuous colorism of the Flemish and Dutch schools. After him the whole direction of English painting was changed in favor of an intellectual ideal of beauty whose source was in the art of the Italian high Renaissance. That English artists did not prove equal to such a change, that their native sensuousness, while never too robust, was stifled by an abject respect for a dematerialized ideal beauty, is largely the fault of Reynolds and the conditions of taste and patronage which he represented and did much to make permanent. There were artists who struggled against his dominating influence, and some of these are considered among the great today. But in the main his influence was disastrous. The advantage passed to France in the early 19th century, and English art is only recently showing signs of recovery.

With the devil painted so black we might be justified in refusing to watch him in action. But, let the reader be reassured; devils have an annoying habit of being impressive and amusing—that is their attraction for the innocent, and Reynolds is no exception.

First we may look briefly at an outline of his career. He was born in Plympton, Devon, in 1723. He entered Thomas Hudson's studio in 1741, remaining there until 1743. Hudson, the most successful artist of the 1740's in England, was a stiff, laborious portrait painter in the tradition of Lely and Kneller. Reynolds left his studio before his legal period of apprenticeship had expired, and painted on his own between 1743 and 1749. In the latter year he went to Italy for three years' study, returning to London in 1752 to set up a portrait practice. He was a success almost immediately. Appointed first President of the Royal Academy in 1768, he was knighted in 1769 and henceforth his success seemed to know no limits. He made an important journey to Flanders and Holland in 1781, countries whose art he had previously largely neglected in favor of Italy. In 1789 his eyes began to fail and he stopped painting from that year until his death in 1792.

His career presents the formation of an artist, who, recognizing the importance of "respectability" in the conduct of the artist in society, meticulously ordered his study of past masters to glean therefrom the essence of their success in picture making. This learning he applied, with any success, to one kind of picture only—the portrait. The reasons for his choice are clear. The portrait market in his day experienced a tremendous boom.

As the English 18th century commercial class grew in wealth and power, and its members penetrated the ranks of the old nobility, old caste walls were weakened. The result was inevitably a more flexible governing society, and one within which it was possible for individuals of force and initiative to rise, despite their lack of noble blood or their humbleness of origin. The demand for the portrait is intimately bound up with these new conditions of social flexibility. The importance of the portrait at any time as a concrete record or symbol of social position is unquestioned. At this time it gave to those individuals of established reputation continued evidence of their position in the social framework; while to those of uncertain social status, those climbing the ladder, it gave an external assurance of progress. Those newly rich, those newly conscious of power and position had their self-esteem considerably buttressed by a properly elevated representation of their persons at the hands of the best, or most fashionable, painter they could afford. Hogarth in the first half of the century had the courage, as we have seen, to counter the rising tide of this demand for the Society portrait. However, by the second half of the century the demand had grown so great that most artists were tempted to devote all their time to portrait painting. Reynolds could not resist the fortune that was waiting to his hand.

Realizing shrewdly the limitations of a portraiture bound to the taste of the patron, he sought to place the artist in England, or at least himself, on a social footing of comparative equality with his well-born or well-moneyed clients. In his view, where previously the English artist (in contrast to a great foreign visitor like Van Dyck) had pandered to the patron, the patron should now pander to the artist. To this extent Reynolds reflects the rising spirit of individualism which Hogarth had represented. But there the resemblance stops. Where Hogarth attempted to break new ground, to strike out in original directions foreshadowing some of the practices of 19th century art, Reynolds was content to look behind him in a spirit of emulation rather than competition.

He early grasped the fact that to control patronage he must produce a portrait which varied from patron to patron. Thereby the quality of uniqueness in each portrait design would of itself tend to sell his work and also give him the right to keep his prices high; at a point, in fact, where his income was such that he need not pot-boil, while at the same time the very expensiveness of a portrait by him, as compared with one by Gainsborough, or still cheaper, Romney, would automatically earn him at least the money-minded respect of the patronage of his day. (It should be noted, also, that he accepted the portrait as the kind of picture most in demand in England. While he regretted this national prejudice, he shrewdly compromised with it in practice, however much he encouraged younger artists to do otherwise.)

The variety and uniqueness of his portrait designs were almost altogether dependent upon his three years' study in Italy, and his visit later to Flanders and Holland. He accumulated in his travels all that he felt was of value in the work of those old masters who were either respected or in fashion in the England of his day. He made no original discoveries for himself in the art of the past. Original discovery might have endangered the reputation he was attempting to build up. The accepted past consisted for the most part of the ideal classicism of Raphael, the " noble " conceptions of Michelangelo, the great Venetian colorists Titian, Tintoretto, and Veronese, and the academic classicism of the Bolognese Carracci and their followers. By a process of assimilation of this heterogeneous group of styles, Reynolds arrived at something of an eclectic style of his own. The style which he sponsored, however, in his *Discourses*, the so-called " Grand Style," the twin gods of which might be said to be Michelangelo and Raphael, is the key to most of his production.

His first portraits before going to Italy are, on the whole, undistinguished. They follow closely the rather heavy metallic surface modeling of his master Hudson. While in Italy he was too busy observing and noting down ideas from the works of other men to do much independent painting of his own. All we know from this period, in fact, that can be surely dated are a few playful caricatures of English travelers, in the manner of Thomas Patch, a fellow Englishman who made his living in Rome in this way. The *Parody of Raphael's " School of Athens "* (Plate 9 a) is the most interesting and amusing of these. Its playfulness and the very fact that it is a parody of Raphael denotes a Reynolds not yet weighed down with a sense of his own importance.

Immediately after his return from Italy there are indications also that his armor of respectability was not yet impervious to some uncontrolled sentiment: witness his portrait of *Horace Walpole*, in the Marchioness of Lansdowne's collection, painted in 1756, with its sensitive, if somewhat uncertain attenuation of form; and the *Lady Betty Hamilton* (Plate 9 b) of 1758 in the Widener collection, Philadelphia. The latter is remarkable both for its delicate characterization and, in contrast to the artist's later generalizations, the relatively firm modeling of the figure and the rendering of detail in the painting of the costume. The generally accepted masterpiece, however, of these first years after Italy is the portrait of *Nelly O'Brien* (Plate 9 c), painted about 1762, and now in the Wallace Collection, London. It marks the end of a period. There is perhaps more direct personal feeling in this portrait than anything Reynolds ever did, and that may explain much of what can only be called its charm.

From the early 1760's on the fruit of his study in Italy comes clearly into view. His emulation of what he calls the " Great or

Grand Style" becomes an all absorbing preoccupation. In his analysis of this style, in the third *Discourse*, he says:

The wish of the genuine painter must be . . . instead of endeavouring to amuse mankind with the minute neatness of his imitations, he must endeavour to improve them by the grandeur of his ideas; instead of seeking praise by deceiving the superficial sense of the spectator, he must strive for fame, by captivating the imagination. . . . This great ideal perfection and beauty are not to be sought in the heavens, but upon the earth. They are about us, and upon every side of us. But the power of discovering what is deformed in nature, or in other words, what is particular and uncommon, can be acquired only by experience; and the whole beauty and grandeur of the art consists, in my opinion, in being able to get above all singular forms, local customs, particularities, and details of every kind.

In the Renaissance theory from which Reynolds derives these ideas (and almost all his ideas in the *Discourses*), history or imaginative painting (which in practice meant usually pictures with mythological or religious subjects) was considered the ideal and highest branch of art, since it was of necessity furthest removed from the documentation of a particularized nature. And by the same token, portraiture and landscape were placed lowest in the artistic scale, since the actual appearance of a sitter or the particularities of a view were felt to be necessary factors in their representation. Reynolds was thus faced with a dilemma. He might wish to paint nothing but history pictures, but his public—unconsciously wise so far as he was concerned—demanded portraits. He got around the difficulty in the following way. In the fourth *Discourse*, he says:

. . . If a portrait-painter is desirous to raise and improve his subject, he has no other means than by approaching it to a general idea. He leaves out all the minute breaks and peculiarities in the face, and changes the dress from a temporary fashion to one more permanent, which has annexed to it no ideas of meanness from its being familiar to us. But [and here Reynolds sees the major difficulty of his method of fusion] if an exact resemblance of an individual be considered as the sole object to be aimed at, the portrait-painter will be apt to lose more than he gains by the acquired dignity taken from general nature. It is very difficult to ennoble the character of a countenance but at the expense of the likeness, which is what is most generally required by such as sit to the painter.

There is perhaps a note of bitterness in that last sentence. Reynolds did suffer the indignity of having portraits returned to him because they were not sufficiently like the sitters. Whether this was his experience with an early essay in the " grand style," the portrait of *Mary, Duchess of Ancaster*, painted in 1764, it is of course impossible to say. The lady wears a would-be antique dress and sandals. Her pose and costume are intended to call up the grandeur of a goddess, but the total result is far from satisfactory. Even less convincing is the Art Institute of Chicago's *Lady Sarah Bunbury Sacrificing to the Graces* (Plate 10 b) of the following year. The picture is certainly not a good portrait in any possible meaning of the word, and Lady Sarah is most certainly not an antique heroine, as her uncertain expression and gestures all too clearly prove.

But Reynolds was not always so unsuccessful in his efforts to raise portraiture to a level above a mean likeness. The *Lady Sarah Bunbury* is simply an indication that he had not completely assimilated some model from the past on which he was basing his design. The adaptation of past masters' compositions for portrait purposes was a cardinal point in the system of teaching he sponsored at the Royal Academy schools. In this connection here is what he tells the students, in the fifteenth *Discourse*:

. . . I would recommend to the young artist when he first attempts invention . . . to select every figure, if possible, from the inventions of Michael Angelo. If such borrowed figures will not bend to his purpose, and he is constrained to make a change to supply a figure himself, that figure will necessarily be in the same style with the rest; and his taste will by this means be naturally initiated, and nursed in the lap of grandeur. He will sooner perceive what constitutes this grand style by one practical trial than by a thousand speculations, and he will in some sort procure to himself that advantage which in these later ages has been denied him, the advantage of having the greatest of artists for his master and instructor.

The next lesson should be, to change the purpose of the figures without changing the attitude, as Tintoret has done with the Samson of Michael Angelo. Instead of the figure which Samson bestrides, he has placed an eagle under him; and instead of the jaw-bone, thunder and lightning in his right hand; and thus it becomes a Jupiter. Titian, in the same manner, has taken the figure which represents God dividing the light from the darkness in the vault of the Capella Sestina, and has introduced it in the famous Battle of Cadore, so much celebrated by Vasari; and, extraordinary as it may seem, it is here converted to a general falling from his horse.

Before the delivery of the above passage Reynolds had long since shown the way by his sometimes merely clever, sometimes wholly successful, example. *The Graces Adorning a Term of Hymen* (Plate 11 a), a portrait of the daughters of Sir William Montgomery, painted in 1774, is one of his cleverest translations. Freely adapted from Nicolas Poussin's *Bacchanalian Dance* (Plate 11 b), in the National Gallery, London, it has an exciting figural rhythm and a splendid pattern of light and shade, both of which are Reynolds' own contribution. But, it must be said, nevertheless, Poussin has not been improved upon.

One point is pertinent here. By such borrowing and transformations Reynolds did not expect that all his public would be deluded into thinking that his many different portrait designs were his own inventions. He knew and expected the learned connoisseurs to see beyond his picture to its source. He was sufficiently flattered if the critics praised the " rightness " or the cleverness of his adaptations. He could not, for example, expect to deceive many people with his portrait of the actress *Mrs. Siddons as the Tragic Muse* (Plate 12 a), in the Huntington Art Gallery, California. Her pose and the little furies behind her throne are too clearly adapted from similar characteristics in Michelangelo's *Prophet Isaiah* (Plate 12 b) on the Sistine Ceiling. But, the source recognized, what Reynolds made of it was sufficiently impressive at times to quiet any accusation of mere plagiarism. Of course, when he failed in his purpose he ran the risk of being laughed at. *Mrs. Billington as St. Cecilia* (Plate 10 a), in the New York Public Library, painted at the very end of his career, is in this category. Inspired partly by Rubens, and perhaps by Raphael's *St. Cecilia* at Bologna, it is none the less so humorlessly pretentious as to border on the ridiculous. The lady's name, in this saintly connection, does not help to improve the situation.

Reynolds did not believe in always borrowing ideas from past masters. In the fifteenth *Discourse* he lectures the Academy students as follows:

When the student has been habituated to this grand conception of the art, when the relish for this style is established, made a part of himself, and is woven into his mind, he will, by this time, have got a power of selecting from whatever occurs in nature that is grand, and corresponds with that taste which he has now acquired; and will pass over whatever is commonplace and insipid. He may then bring to the mart such works of his own proper invention as may enrich and increase the general stock of invention in our art.

A number of Reynolds' portraits show his own learned originality. It is to be found, for example, in the *Jane, Countess of Harrington* (Plate 12 c), in the Huntington Art Gallery, *Mrs. Elizabeth Carnac*, in the Wallace Collection, and *Lady Elizabeth Delmé and her Children*, in the National Gallery, Washington. All three present a " grand " rhetorical effect. This is not to say, however, that they are profound portraits, either in a formal or a psychological way. The noble gesture, the splendid flow of drapery are, after all, an outward show. Such rhetoric on extended examination proves a trifle hollow, for one thing because it is not sufficiently realized in its formal expression. As for psychological penetration, we must not expect to find such a thing within the confines of the ideal portraiture at which the artist is aiming.

Within this ideal, also, there is little place for the intimate portrait. Even the *Duchess of Devonshire and her Child*, at Chatsworth, light in temper though it pretends to be, is still on the " grand " side. One might expect a note of intimacy in portraits of children, but here Reynolds' idealizing propensity was too much to the fore (he was a bachelor) to allow him to record the awkward reality of childhood—a reality which Goya, and even Hogarth on occasion, in their portraits of children have discerned. *Miss Frances Crewe* (Plate 10 c), in the Marquess of Crewe's collection, London, is as close as Reynolds ever came to a truly individual treatment of a child. But even here he cannot forget his ideal of child innocence and Miss Crewe herself, as a result, has escaped him. His most amusing child portrait is that of the

[21]

brother of this little girl, *Master Crewe* (Plate 10 d)—dressed and posed as Henry VIII. The parody on Holbein and the King is witty, but here again the child himself is lost in the fun.

Interestingly enough the hollowness at the core of Reynolds' " ideal beauty," when it is applied to women and children, does not appear to have spoiled his portraits of men. The artifice of his ideal style, it would seem, needed a masculine base to give it substance. An ideal style joined to an ideal of femininity or child-hood tended to take the body out of all three. In the portrait of *Dr. Samuel Johnson* (Plate 13 a), Tate Gallery, London, Reynolds' idealizing generalizations are at a minimum and in their place we have a penetrating analysis of character which would do credit to Rembrandt. Here is all the weighty, cantankerous gran-deur of the man himself as we know him from countless Boswell anecdotes. A pen and ink portrait of *Oliver Goldsmith* (Plate 13 b) in the British Museum is another powerful character study. It is, by the way, one of the few drawings by Reynolds in existence and perhaps the only one of any value. He did not take kindly to pen or pencil, unfortunately, and the discipline which such execution demanded. He preferred to draw with the brush directly on the canvas—a practice which, because of his uncertain sense of formal structure, results only too often in a boneless articulation of his figures. He covers up his weakness very often with a fine display of color and design, but it is present nevertheless and will always remain a disturbing feature of his work, particularly for those who observe him closely and long.

The Johnson and Goldsmith portraits are essentially studies in personality—both were intimate friends of the artist. In most of his portraits of men of position, however—statesmen, church-men, soldiers, sailors—Reynolds has a happy faculty of identifying the man with his position. This, of course, is another use of the " grand manner." Where a lady had been raised above a parti-cular level and given at times the air of a goddess, an admiral like *Lord Heathfield* (Plate 14 b), in the National Gallery, London, is made more masculine and imposing by a merging of his individuality with his role of victorious captor of Gibraltar.

The Heathfield portrait and others of the same caliber, such as that of the *Hon. Augustus Keppel* in the National Maritime Museum, Greenwich, might be considered justification enough of all Reynolds' theories of the grand style—did they stand alone. Unfortunately for his future reputation, he did not stop with portraits. To justify his preaching he was forced—perhaps against his better judgment—to attempt an occasional subject or history picture. His colossal failure in almost every one of these would not be so important (other men have failed in some department of their art) had he not stressed in almost every *Discourse* the lesser importance of the portrait beside the picture of imaginative invention. If he had not written a line or delivered himself of a public lecture, one feels, his influence would perhaps have been less pernicious. But the difference between his theory and his practice is so great that when we look at, say, his *Death of Cardinal Beaufort* (Plate 14 c) in the Dulwich Gallery, we are appalled by the artist's want of emotional control; or rather his want of imaginative emotion altogether, for what is here is a fake. Holywood of 1910 could not improve on its ridiculousness. One realizes from such a performance—and it is very typical—that despite all of Reynolds' high-sounding theories of the appeal of ideal art to the imagination, he himself was only safe from a fatuous sentimentality—and not always then—when he was faced with the compelling reality of an individual sitter. The portrait in his scheme might be raised above mere face-painting to picture making, but the positive personality of a living client—when he was forced to realize it in part at least—was his chief protection against the silly and bathetic.

We conclude, then, as we began: it is one of the tragedies of English painting as a school that the essential weakness of the academic method which Reynolds inspired and furthered has gone so long uncontested by all but a few painters and theorists in England. And these have been too few, too weak, or the disease is too deep-seated to alter in the least the practice of the Royal Academy even down to the present day.

CHAPTER III

THOMAS GAINSBOROUGH

In discussing Hogarth and Reynolds there has been implicit in our measure of their independence or acceptance of the fashionable taste of their day their attitude toward the English portrait mania. Hogarth, we have seen, while he never stopped portrait painting, gave it, on the whole, the least of his attention. Reynolds, while outwardly deploring its meanness and limitations as an art form, nevertheless accepted it with some modification, because of public demand. Gainsborough's case is rather different. He began as a landscape painter and throughout his life landscape painting remained his first love, if he did not always make it his first interest. His marriage of landscape to portraiture was one of convenience, and the progeny, while sometimes extraordinarily happy, was on occasion pretty anemic. He produced too much because unquestionably he was the victim of circumstances. He had apparently a strong-willed wife and two demanding daughters. A large income was necessary to keep all three and, to make matters more difficult, he had none of Reynolds' business acumen to help him husband his artistic and financial resources. The portrait paid and portraits he painted—divinely, expertly, and when energy or inspiration were wanting, at least dexterously. He did not put up Hogarth's fierce struggle for artistic independence. He had none of his Cockney belligerence. He did, however, attempt to make the best of a difficult situation, and he kept his landscape painting alive, somehow, although he is said never to have sold a landscape. Here alone is a mark of his own peculiar independence of spirit, and one which singles him out as one of the forerunners of the great landscape art of the 19th century.

Gainsborough, one may say, came to landscape painting naturally. The city-bred social critic Hogarth never gave it a thought, except as a background to some of his out-of-door conversation pieces.

[24]

Reynolds, following classical art theory, placed it, when separated from history painting, on a level with portraiture and, having sought to elevate the one, he considered it either impossible or beyond him to dignify the other. Gainsborough, country-born (1727) and undisturbed by theory of any sort, went as a boy on sketching expeditions through the fields and woods around his native Sudbury. At an early age he came in contact with examples of Dutch landscape in local collections of pictures, and Dutch naturalism from the beginning directed the formation of his own early style. His first known work, *Cornard Wood*, in the National Gallery, London, begun by his own account before he was fourteen and finished when he was nineteen, shows this strong Dutch influence. The presence of numerous Dutch pictures locally is not surprising when it is remembered that this eastern region of England had close commercial connections with Dutch and Flemish ports. Perhaps too, because of some similarity in climate and character of country between this part of England and Holland, local English patrons found Dutch landscape immediately attractive.

A strong grasp of three-dimensional space is an outstanding feature of the work of such painters as Hobbema, Ruisdael, and Wynants, and it is this quality of spatial depth that Gainsborough successfully repeats, so early in his career, in his view of *Cornard Wood* (Plate 15 a). It might be compared with a Hobbema, for example the so-called *Holford Landscape* (Plate 15 b), in the National Gallery, Washington. In the latter picture one notes the conventional tufted foliage, the winding cart road leading the eye into the picture and carrying it into the distance; the careful spatial division of the whole scene; the foreground in shadow, marked by two figures to the right, and the greatest massing of foliage on the left; the middle ground under a strong light, with figures on the road to the left, and the narrow strip of horizon. In the *Cornard Wood* we have again the tufted foliage, the figures in the middle ground, the strip of horizon. But there is a major difference. The lighting has changed. Where Hobbema somewhat artificially spotlights the middle ground, the light here streams into the picture from the left, picking out in its path tree trunks and figures and the patch of grassy bank in the foreground. The result is more natural in effect, and this touch of greater naturalism, in deference to some particular quality of lighting which the artist had noted, is Gainsborough's significant contribution to an otherwise very traditional Dutch treatment of the scene as a whole.

The early sketches for *Cornard Wood* (it seems difficult to believe a boy not yet fourteen could have done more) must have shown considerable promise. On leaving school at fourteen, he was sent to London to study, where he remained until he was eighteen or nineteen. This early London period is practically blank so far as any record of his activities is concerned. He appears to have studied under Hubert Gravelot, a French artist chiefly noted for his book illustrations, and Francis Hayman, an English artist of considerable repute in the 1740's. No certain work of Gainsborough's from this student period survives aside from *Cornard Wood*, at which he probably worked intermittently. Returning to Sudbury about 1745, for the next seven years he seems to have occupied himself with landscape studies, still in the Dutch tradition. About 1752 he moved with his wife and two children to Ipswich, a larger town north of Sudbury, and made a beginning upon a serious portrait practice. It is during this period that he developed a type of picture combining portrait and landscape which is the chief glory of his early career. *Mr. and Mrs. Andrews* (Plate 16 a) is in many ways the best of its kind. With this work, and others like it, Gainsborough shows his first real advance toward an independent style. In the so-called conversation piece as painted by Hogarth, Zoffany, and Gainsborough's London master Hayman, portrait figures were often grouped out of doors. In such pictures, for example Hayman's *Children of Jonathan Tyers* (Plate 16 b), which Gainsborough may have seen painted, the landscape is simply a flat conventional studio backdrop with little or no relation to nature. The gestures of the boy holding the pheasant, and the girl standing, are somewhat mannered, and the diagonal tree trunk is used obviously to tie the group together. If similar features are compared in the *Mr. and Mrs. Andrews* it will be seen at once how Gainsborough has shed in one stroke all the studio artifice of the Hayman tradition, and out of an old form made something completely new. It is a picture thoroughly fresh and natural from almost every point of view. The figures are still grouped before a tree, but, in contrast to Hayman's, they are most naturally posed, with not the slightest hint of forced gestures. The placing of the figures to one side of a long narrow landscape is a quite original compositional scheme. The balance established between the figures on the one hand, and the trees and sheaves of wheat on the other, is extremely delicate. The lighting of the figures, throwing their contours into a sharp relief, compensates for the greater spatial emphasis given to the landscape to the right. Dutch landscape conventions still remain, but they have now been used in a personal, completely assimilated, manner. For the winding road convention Gainsborough substitutes rows of wheat, which as before carry the eye into the composition. The whole scene is more open, more enveloped by light and air than *Cornard Wood*. It is in many ways an inspired performance. In its naturalness of landscape approach and, as a portrait, its direct grasp of character, in gesture and expression, it is the masterpiece of his Ipswich period, and the equal in its way of the best work of his maturity.

The compositional type of which this is the prime example is unfortunately one from which Gainsborough broke away in the late 1750's. Portrait commissions were increasing and their urgency could not be denied. The even compromise between portrait and landscape which the Andrews picture represents involved no doubt an expenditure of effort not warranted by the price received, particularly if a similar price could be had for a more conventional portrait when the figure was seen close-up, so to speak, rather than at a distance. The change towards a greater concentration on the figure itself may be observed in the Frick Collection's *Lady Innes* (Plate 17 a), painted about 1757. The landscape is relegated to a subsidiary position. The naive charm and exquisite modeling which are so characteristic of the Andrews picture are here writ large. The consummate grace of line in the firm, subtly sculptured head and hands, is combined with a nervous flutter of excitement in the ripples of satin and the cascades of lace flounces at the sleeves. The landscape background is a brilliantly suggestive scribble, nothing more—an idealized massing of foliage and sky in soft focus, acting simply as a counterfoil to the sharp contours of the figure. The rose bush to the left, and the rose held gracefully in the lady's hand are, with the figure, the only objects rendered with a sharpness and precision which reveal direct observation of nature. With splendid directness the painter has caught the mood and emotional tone of the subject.

Similarly, in *The Painter's Daughters* (Plate 17 b), in the Tate Gallery, London, painted about the same year as the *Lady Innes,* there is present an instantaneity of vision, catching in gesture and expression the incisive look of a characteristic moment, which is to mark all the artist's best work. Even in its unfinished condition this must be one of the most delightful studies of children from the brush of any artist. How much more convincing it is in its insight into the child temper than Reynolds' fancied ideal innocence.

Leaving this period of almost instinctive naturalism, it is perhaps something of a shock when we come, over ten years later, to the artifice of *The Blue Boy,* painted probably in Bath about 1769. Gainsborough's removal there in 1759 was made on the advice of his most interested Ipswich patron, Phillip Thicknesse. From a portrait standpoint the advice was good, for Bath was the center during the season of the most fashionable social life of England. Aside from a tremendously increased production of portraits, for he quickly became the most sought-after painter of the town, the artist was brought into contact at this time with the work of Van Dyck, in the great collection of pictures at Wilton House, near Bath. The copying and close study of some of the best works of that master of the Society portrait was of tremendous influence in bringing Gainsborough's style to the mature and effortless brilliance of execution with which we are most familiar. *The Blue Boy* (Plate 18 a), now in the Huntington Art Gallery,

California, is the most obvious result of this Van Dyck study. In costume, composition, and paint, it is a masterful adaptation of the older master's manner; the fluid pattern of satin folds in the costume, the dazzling brilliance of light and shade, the noble dignity of pose and facial expression, all bespeak their origin. But certainly this, and other portraits of this time, such as *Captain Wade* and *Benjamin Truman* (Plate 18 b), are not slavish copies of Van Dyck; they are rather indications of Gainsborough's reverence for his work and an example of how completely he has assimilated and made himself master of one of the best portrait styles of the 17th century. And he has added much that is his own. There is, in the latter two portraits at least, a direct treatment of character, and a complete realization of the figure in a well defined space, which have been part of his genius from the first.

The year 1774 finds him in London after fourteen very successful years in Bath. He was now, so to speak, at the top of his form and in a position to share the honors with Reynolds for the position of foremost painter in England. Before his coming the London art world was acquainted with his work. The Royal Academy included Gainsborough in its roster of thirty-six founder members. Each year, therefore, he sent up his quota of pictures to the annual Academy exhibition. In 1773 he stopped hanging pictures there, the result, apparently, of a squabble with Reynolds over a picture the latter refused to accept for exhibition. In 1777, however, he reappeared on the Academy walls with what is popularly considered to be his masterpiece in feminine portraiture, *Mrs. Graham* (Plate 19 a), now in the National Gallery of Scotland. Here the sheer virtuosity of painting, particularly in the red satin of the dress, and the masterful poise of the figure, are most remarkable. To the lady's own natural beauty Gainsborough has added an elegance and dignity of pose and composition which gives the whole a magnificent air. The ease and nobility of manner which he conveys has seldom been equaled.

At about this time he painted the *Miss Frances Duncombe* (Plate 19 b), in the Frick Collection. The result, one must admit, is not quite so monumentally successful. The crossed arms, one hand holding the hat, produces a noticeable break in the vertical sweep of the figure. The trees and monument to the left are a trifle heavy in relation to the figure, as compared with the lightness and economy of the column support in the portrait of *Mrs. Graham.* But if the *Miss Duncombe* here falls somewhat short, there are undoubted compensations in the paintings of the blue satin dress and the graceful, lightly poised figure, which finds an echo in the feathery trees in the background.

The delicate relation of landscape to figure which we have noted in the early Ipswich group portraits is brought, in these later works, to a balance so perfectly adjusted, further progress in this direction is almost unthinkable. A Reynolds portrait in the grand manner, such as his *Jane, Countess of Harrington* (Plate 12 c), is by comparison heavy and theatrical. It has an unmistakable grandeur, of course, but the basis of feeling is a prosaic, or shall we say a rationalized rhetoric, however noble in intention. The basis of Gainsborough's expression is sentiment, rather than reason; it is also poetic, a distillation of the facts of normal experience to a point where they take on a greater than normal significance. Nowhere is this difference in the mental and emotional outlook of Reynolds and Gainsborough more strikingly revealed than by a comparison of their portraits of the same subject, *Mrs. Siddons* (Plates 12 a and 21 b) ; the one elegant and grand, but superbly natural nevertheless, the other artificial, in the best sense of the word, and theatrical, as befitted an ideal characterization of a great tragedienne.

Gainsborough's *Mrs. Siddons* dates from the last years of his life. He died in 1788. In his last twenty-eight years, equally divided between Bath and London, the insistent demands of a steadily increasing portrait practice left little time for his first passion—landscape painting. He had begun, as we have seen, in the Dutch naturalistic tradition, but in the meantime his contact with fashionable taste in Bath and London produced an important change. The so-called picturesque-classical landscape was the first to make its influence felt on polite English taste, for the reason that this style combined certain literary and intellectual associations which appealed to poets, writers, and connoisseurs in England during the major part of the 18th century. In fact such poets as Pope and Thomson in describing a view or a landscape setting drew their images not from nature, as a rule, but from paintings. The pictures of Claude Lorrain, Gaspard Poussin, and Salvator Rosa were their chief inspiration. And, curiously enough, the influence of such painters was projected back through English poets to English painters, Gainsborough among them, the claims of poetry upon public or cultivated attention having always been greater in England than those of the pictorial arts.

The " picturesque," it should be noted, is the very antithisis of the natural. In a way it is a parallel in landscape painting of the grand style in portraiture, as practiced by Reynolds, and both derive from a classical non-particularizing ideal. But just as Reynolds' grand style contains overtones of a personal rhetorical sort, so the picturesque landscapes of Claude and Rosa were a kind of watering down of the intellectualized architectural order of the purer classicism of Nicolas Poussin. In both the classical and pseudo-classical traditions, the chief interest was in abstract picture-making, and the choice or adaptation of scenery to express certain moods harmonious with a story, usually from antique history or legend. The picturesque artist sought, however, to stress the emotional, even romantic elements in a scene—sometimes out of all proportion to the story. Ruins, rivers, torrents, mountains, unlimited plains, or seas stretching to the far horizon— these were his stock in trade, the instruments to express his various moods. Rosa specialized in what might be called the romance of violence in nature—the terrible and sublime—as did Gaspard Poussin, on occasion. Claude, on the other hand, explored the emotional possibilities of peaceful, pastoral distances and the sweet sad thought of an antique world long past.

This kind of landscape, made popular, as we have said, by English poets, had an additional attraction for cultivated, or would-be cultivated, Englishmen. Many of them had gone to Italy on the Grand Tour. They desired some record of their visit, and the romantic associations called up by the picturesque painters fitted their needs when they returned home. They either bought such pictures in Italy or London. The latter market was flooded with originals of, or copies after, Claude, Gaspard, and Rosa and, in fact, if one could not go to Italy, or did not care to, the equivalent of such a journey was ready to one's eyes in picture after picture.

What of the English landscape painter faced with such a taste? His native heath, as Richard Wilson discovered, did not at first call up the fine Italian mood, and hence he was forced, as he thought, to go to Italy to paint the familiar Roman Campagna. That he did not succeed in selling many of his canvases, however, is understandable. The competition with Claudes and Rosas was too keen. Why buy an English edition if one could as easily procure an Italian original? But to live at all, however poorly, the English landscapist had to follow the fashion and this Wilson did, with some later modification, until his death. Likewise Gainsborough, when he came to Bath, must have discovered that there was no market for his naturalistic, Dutch influenced, Ipswich landscapes, and he too succumbed to the picturesque craze. He did so perhaps the more willingly since a thriving portrait practice kept him studio-bound and those youthful rambles through the countryside were now less and less possible. The picturesque with all its imaginative, unreal characteristics was, therefore, a way out of his personal dilemma. He wanted to continue landscape painting while painting portraits. Here was a style which was both fashionable and—like Reynolds' portraits—so bound to pictures rather than to nature that anyone with sufficient energy and technical dexterity could paint any number of landscapes without ever having to expose himself to a real landscape of any kind.

He turned, then, to sketching imaginary compositions. The number of these shorthand charcoal scribbles which exist is almost countless. The best of them are but brilliant suggestions and appear to have been dashed off in a few minutes (Plate 20 a). One readily detects the picturesque formula in their easy juggling of foliage, hill, and rustic figure. The urgent stimulus to explore new landscape problems is gone. The freshness of the Ipswich period is now only a memory. *The Bridge* (Plate 20 b), in the

Tate Gallery, painted *ca.* 1777, is only an elaborate restatement of the once carefully noted undulation of hill and bank in the Andrews portrait. The "sublime" sweep of mountain and the artificially emotive patches of lighting are no more than a brilliant reshuffling of effects once intimately experienced and now turned into a highly developed convention.

Together with this sentimental treatment of landscape, and in the same picturesque tradition, Gainsborough developed a rustic genre picture which, while it has Flemish and Dutch derivations, has been regarded recently as a distinctive pre-Wordsworthian expression of English naturalism.[1] *The Market Cart*, in the London National Gallery, *The Cottage Door*, in the Huntington Art Gallery, and *Rustic Children* (Plate 21 a), in the Tate, are outstanding examples of this type. Such pictures may reflect a genuine sympathy on the part of Gainsborough for what the poet Gray called "the short and simple annals of the poor." But one cannot escape the note of picturesque artifice which they all betray in their overly-ragged peasants and their equally studied settings. It is, therefore, possible to read too much into them. More probably they are a simple extension of the current picturesque fashion and should be so studied, rather than as documents of Gainsborough's personal feelings towards the impoverished countryman.

Such a warning is necessary when one remembers to what heights of refinement Gainsborough finally raised the studio-imagined picturesque. The characteristics of his latest landscapes are their increasingly stylized quality, so far as design is concerned, and they share with the progress of his portraiture a steadily mounting complexity of rhythm and delicacy of brush-work and a more and more decorative use of color, as opposed to any naturalistic intention.

Just before his death, in a small group of pictures, he takes this landscape and, with the greatest artifice, combines it with figures to form an altogether new type of picture. *The Morning Walk*,

---

[1] Chauncey B. Tinker, *Painter and Poet* (Cambridge: Harvard University Press, 1938), chap. IV.

or *Squire Hallett and His Wife* (Plate 22 a) as it is otherwise known (1785), shows a late step in the development of this kind of aristocratic, as opposed to peasant, genre. Figures in movement, on first analysis, appear to be the chief characteristic of this new order of things. An earlier drawing of about 1780, *A Lady Walking in the Mall,* in the British Museum, is one of the first indications of this trend. *The Mall in St. James's Park* (Plate 22 b), in the Frick Collection, is the most elaborate expression of this poetry of movement which, if Gainsborough had lived to develop it further, might have produced results to rival Watteau's exquisitely languorous *fête galantes.* The rhythmic flutter of light and movement which pulses through the whole scene is the final expression of a sensibility tuned to a pitch more subtle and inspired than that of any other artist in the history of English painting.

With each doll-like figure in *The Mall* treated as a note in a series of coloristic chords and rhythmic patterns, one is reminded forcibly of Gainsborough's passion for music. He was an amateur musician, a collector of violins and viols-da-gamba, and he preferred the company of musicians to that of the intellectual and fashionable world of the day—in contrast to Reynolds who chose to mingle only with the most respected members of society. In this connection a series of letters which Gainsborough wrote to a musician friend, William Jackson of Exeter, reveals more of his personality than any biographer can ever hope to express. One of these letters will provide a fitting conclusion to this short study.

Bath, June 4th

My dear Jackson,

    I am much obliged to you for your last letter, and the lessons received before. I think I now begin to see a little into the nature of modulation and the introduction of flats and sharps; and when we meet you shall hear me play extempore. My friend Abel has been to visit me, but he made but a short stay, being obliged to go to Paris for a month or six weeks, after which he promised to come again. There never was a poor devil so fond of harmony, with so little knowledge of it; so that what you have done is pure charity. I dined with Mr. Duntze in expectation (and indeed full assurance) of hearing your scholar Miss Flood (?)

play a little, but was for the second time flung. . . . I'm sick of Portraits and wish very much to take my viol-da-gam and walk off to some
sweet village, where I can paint landskips and enjoy the fag end of life
in quietness and ease. But these fine ladies [his daughters] and their
tea drinkings, dancings, husband-huntings, &c. &c. &c., will fob me out
of the last ten years, and I fear miss getting husbands too. But we can
say nothing to these things you know, Jackson, we must jogg on and be
content with the jingling of the bells, only d—— it I hate a dust, the
kicking up of a dust, and being confined in harness to follow the track
whilst others ride in the waggon, under cover, stretching their legs in the
straw at ease, and gazing at green trees and blue skies without half my
taste. That's d——d hard. My comfort is I have five viols-da-gamba,
three Jayes and two Barak Normans.

Adieu,

Tho. Gainsborough.[2]

[2] Published, with eleven other letters to Jackson, in William T. Whitley's
Thomas Gainsborough (London: Smith Elder, 1915), Appendix A.

Chapter IV

WILLIAM BLAKE

The conflict between artist and public which we saw beginning with Hogarth reaches with Blake a point of social and psychological friction which there is no mistaking. His personal idiosyncracies may explain much, on the surface, but the potential democratic, revolutionary state of England and of Europe in the last quarter of the 18th century explains more. Blake was a child of crisis, and this colored not only his life but his art.

He was born in London in 1757 and died there in 1827 at the age of 70. His father was a hosier of fair means, a dissenter from the Church of England, and, what is more important for Blake's development, a reader of the mystical writings of Swedenborg. The child William indicated at an early age certain abnormal propensities of imagination. Blake the elder, after many misgivings, finally realized that he had an unusual, if difficult, child. Finding that the boy resented not only his own beatings and corrections but those of a school, he had him brought up at home without formal education. He was encouraged above all to learn drawing, with the curious result, as one biographer has noted, that " he became a poet and later learned several living and dead languages." [1]

At the age of ten he was sent to a drawing school where he was taught to draw from casts of antique sculpture in the accepted academic practice of the time. He had previously studied the beauties of high Renaissance figure drawings in prints after such old masters as Raphael and Michelangelo. It should be emphasized, however, that the style of these masters came to him in a diluted form, in prints, at one remove from the originals. He never visited Italy. It is, in fact, this early study of prints and his

[1] Alan Clutton-Brock, *Blake* (New York, The MacMillan Company, 1933), p. 12.

continued use of these throughout the impressionable years of his studentship which in part explains his life-long weakness in exact anatomical rendering of the human body. It is nevertheless a weakness he would probably have been the first to admit, when stated as baldly as we have done, holding as he did in nothing but contempt the laborious imitation of materialistic reality. What appealed to him in these prints after Raphael and Michelangelo, and in others after Dürer and the German school, was their clear definition in outline, which, of course, was exaggerated in the process of engraving. Compare for example, his *Creation of Eve*, in the Boston Museum (Plate 23 a), with Michelangelo's in the Sistine Ceiling (Plate 23 b). This linear description of form as opposed to the more or less obliterated outlines of Venetian or later Flemish painting with their emphasis upon coloristic rather than formal values, is at the basis of Blake's style and explains in great part his violent hatred of oil paint, at least in his early years. The paint brush as a drawing instrument he seems always to have abhorred, because he was unable to make with it that precise outline he so fanatically admired and which was only ideally possible through the use of some sharp instrument, be it pencil, pen, or graving tool. On drawing as a basis of painting he writes as follows:

The distinction that is made in modern times between a Painting and Drawing proceeds from ignorance of art. The merit of a Picture is the same as the merit of a Drawing. The dawber dawbs his Drawings; he who draws his Drawings draws his Pictures. There is no difference between Rafael's Cartoons and his Frescos, or Pictures, except that the Frescos, or Pictures, are more finished. When Mr. B. [i. e., Blake] formerly painted in oil colours his Pictures were shewn to certain painters and connoisseurs, who said that they were very admirable Drawings on canvass, but not Pictures; but they said the same of Rafael's Pictures. Mr. B. thought this the greatest of compliments, though it was meant otherwise. If losing and obliterating the outline constitutes a Picture, Mr. B. will never be so foolish as to do one. Such art of losing the outlines is the art of Venice and Flanders; it loses all character, and leaves what some people call expression; but this is a false notion of expression; expression cannot exist without character as its stamina; and neither character nor expression can exist without firm and determinate outline. Fresco Painting is susceptible of higher finishing than Drawing on Paper, or than any other method of Painting. But he must have a strange organisation of sight who does not prefer a Drawing on Paper to a Dawbing in Oil by the same master, supposing both to be done with equal care.

The great and golden rule of art, as well as of life is this; That the more distinct, sharp, and wiry the bounding line, the more perfect the work of art, and the less keen and sharp, the greater is the evidence of weak imitation, plagiarism, and bungling. Great inventors, in all ages knew this; Protogenes and Apelles knew each other by this line. Rafael and Michael Angelo and Albert Dürer are known by this and this alone. The want of this determinate and bounding form evidences the want of idea in the artist's mind, the pretence of the plagiary in all its branches. How do we distinguish the oak from the beech, the horse from the ox, but by the bounding outline? How do we distinguish one face or countenance from another, but by the bounding line and its infinite inflexions and movements? What is it that builds a house and plants a garden, but the definite and determinate? What is it that distinguishes honesty from knavery, but the hard and wiry line of rectitude and certainty in the actions and intentions? Leave out this line, and you leave out life itself; all is chaos again, and the line of the almighty must be drawn out upon it before man or beast can exist. Talk no more then of Correggio, or Rembrandt, or any other of these plagaries of Venice or Flanders. They were but the lame imitators of lines drawn by their predecessors, and their works prove themselves contemptible, disarranged imitations, and blundering, misapplied copies.[2]

Combined with his study of the antique and prints after old masters, a still more important technical influence on his work, above all in the shaping of a congenial vehicle for the expression of his peculiarly personal, imaginative conceptions, was his long and early association with medieval sculpture. It is in this element of his style that he betrays the romantic neo-gothic tendencies of his time, popularized earlier by Horace Walpole at Strawberry Hill. In particular he studied the architectural sculptures of Westminster Abbey, where he spent much of his apprenticeship drawing tombs for an engraving master to whom he had been articled after leaving his first drawing school. He must have seen, for example, the Angels in the triforium of the south transept

[2] Geoffrey Keynes, ed., *Poetry and Prose of William Blake* (The Nonesuch Press, 1932), p. 805.

(Plate 24 b), with their flowing draperies whose folds describe a decorative linear pattern rather than any strictly functional organization of the materials of costume. This is a characteristically medieval approach to reality as opposed to the correct, if idealized, formal and logical organization of masses of drapery in the robe of God the Father in Michaelangelo's *Creation of Eve*. It explains much of the difference in Blake's translation of the latter's design.

The Wise and Foolish Virgins (Plate 24 a), in the Metropolitan Museum (*ca*. 1822), one of his greatest and most moving designs, should be compared also with the Westminister Angels for a similar organization of clinging draperies and linear rhythms. It should be noted here that the Gothic is really a sort of catalytic agent which with Blake changes the antique and high Renaissance styles into something quite personal and mystical—just as, in another way, with Greco a combination of Venetian colorism, Byzantine formalism, and Michelangelesque mannerism is fused into a medium for the expression of Spanish mysticism.

These examples of Blake in which the two principal technical influences upon his style may be observed have been chosen from among his late designs for the purpose of illustration. They are designs which show his finished adaptation of classical and medieval modes of representation.

In his very early work he shows a more timidly correct copying of the accepted forms of classical design, in such a history picture as *The Penance of Jane Shore* (Plate 25 a), dating from the 1780's, in the Robertson collection in England. This drawing is marked by little or none of the later characteristics of his work and perhaps only in the peculiarly fluid linear draperies can one readily detect his hand. The same is true of his classico-academic illustrations of the Joseph story in the Fitzwilliam Museum, Cambridge, with their strange overtone of non-classic unrestrained emotion.

A few years later, about 1795, Blake approaches a more strictly personal emotional effect in a subject perhaps better suited to the quality of his linear, pulsating style—*Oberon and Titania Asleep on a Lily Petal* from the "Song of Los" (Plate 25 b). There is the same child-like innocent quality in this illustration that we find in such a poem as his " Little Lamb, who made thee? " Here is, too, the most important emotive element in his imaginative designs, despite his theories of line—his superb use of color in transparent washes or opaque patches, usually red, yellow, or blue. With this illustration we cross the line dividing Blake from the work of the general run of his contemporaries in the second half of the 18th century. It should be recalled that during these years when the *Jane Shore* and *Oberon* drawings were produced, Blake was making a fairly comfortable living as a professional engraver of other men's work and he continued engraving either his own or others' designs for the rest of his life, whenever he could get commissions. Engraving was his trade, in effect, and during the first half of his life, at least, that is until about 1800, he was often so occupied with his engraving tools he could only spend time on his own work in the evenings.

He early showed himself inclined to watercolor drawings rather than oils as a means of personal expression because, as we have already pointed out, his ruling passion was for line drawing washed with watercolor rather than obliterated with oil. He not only preferred drawing to oil painting, he evolved, as we have seen, an almost mystical defense of his technique. He openly despised, then, the rational examination of a universalized nature which the academic taste of his time considered a basis of all art study. Despite the admiration for Raphael and Michelangelo which he held in common with members of the Royal Academy, he saw the purity and classic precision of Roman and Florentine art wholly in terms of a containing outline—an outline which to him served to give expression to an imaginative and quite immaterial idea. The academic admirers, on the other hand, looked upon Raphael and Michelangelo as the greatest exponents of an ideal beauty based upon the imitation of the most typical, and hence most perfect, forms in nature. Reynolds in his *Discourses*, as we indicated in a previous chapter, held to the latter view; but Blake despised Reynolds. He annotated a copy of the *Discourses* and the chief burden of his criticism—which is most violent and scurrilous—is against eclecticism and the rational basis of art teaching which it implied. Reynolds, in his view, was not content to praise the ideal grand style of Michelangelo and Raphael; he must try to combine this ideal with the colorism of the Venetians or the chiaroscuro of the Baroque. Such a fusion of imaginative drawing and materialistic color Blake could not stand, and particularly he could not abide Reynolds' frequently contradictory position of praising the grand style, while practicing and condoning something less purely ideal in his own work. In an introductory annotation to the *Discourses*, Blake writes:

I consider Reynolds's Discourses to the Royal Academy as the Simulations of the Hypocrite who smiles particularly where he means to Betray. His Praise of Rafael is like the Hysteric smile of Revenge. His Softness & Candour, the hidden trap & the poisoned feast. He praises Michel Angelo for Qualities which Michel Angelo abhorr'd, & He blames Rafael for the only Qualities which Rafael Valued. Whether Reynolds knew what he was doing is nothing to me: the Mischief is just the same whether a Man does it Ignorantly or Knowingly. I always consider'd True Art & True Artists to be particularly Insulted & Degraded by the Reputation of these Discourses, As much as they were Degraded by the Reputation of Reynolds's Paintings, & that Such Artists as Reynolds are at all times Hired by the Satans for the Depression of Art—A Pretence of Art, To destroy Art.[3]

In the same vein Blake wrote a poem on the self-portrait Reynolds presented to the Florentine Academy and which hangs today in the Uffizi (Plate 14 a).

FLORENTINE INGRATITUDE

Sir Joshua sent his own Portrait to
The birth Place of Michael Angelo,
And in the hand of the simpering fool
He put a dirty paper scroll,
And on the paper, to be polite,
Did " Sketches by Michael Angelo " write.
The Florentines said, " 'Tis a Dutch English bore,
" Michael Angelo's Name writ on Rembrandt's door."

[3] Geoffrey Keynes, ed., *Poetry and Prose of William Blake* (The Nonesuch Press, 1932), p. 979.

[41]

The Florentines call it an English Fetch,
For Michael Angelo did never sketch.
Every line of his has Meaning
And needs neither Suckling nor Weaning.
'Tis the trading English Venetian cant
To speak Michael Angelo & Act Rembrandt.
It will set his Dutch friends all in a roar
To write " Mich. Ang." on Rembrandt's Door.
But You must not bring in your hand a Lie
If you mean the Florentines should buy.
Ghiotto's Circle or Apelles' Line
Were not the Work of Sketchers drunk with Wine,
Nor of the City Clark's warm hearted Fashion,
Nor of Sir Isaac Newton's Calculation,
Nor of the City Clark's Idle Facilities
Which sprang from Sir Isaac Newton's great Abilities.

These Verses were written by a very Envious Man,
Who, whatever likeness he may have to Michael Angelo,
Never can have any to Sir Jehoshuan.[4]

But what insulted Blake's romantic worship of individual genius
in art and the power of inspiration was Reynolds' constant praise
of reason at the expense of imagination in the training of academy
students. Herein we have the essential difference between the
empirical rationalism of Reynolds and the demoniac, inspirational
approach of Blake. Speaking of the third *Discourse*, the latter
says:

A work of Genius is a Work " Not to be obtain'd by the Invocation of
Memory & her Syren Daughters, but by Devout prayer to that Eternal
Spirit, who can enrich with all utterance & knowledge & sends out his
Seraphim with the hallowed fire of his Altar to touch & Purify the lips of
whom he pleases."—MILTON.

The following Discourse is particularly Interesting to Block heads, as
it endevours to prove That there is No such thing as Inspiration & that
any Man of a plain Understanding may by Thieving from Others become
a Mich. Angelo.[5]

Referring to the following passage in the same *Discourse*: " But

---

[4] *Ibid.*, pp. 1016-1017.   [5] *Ibid.*, p. 986.

on this, as upon many other occasions, we ought to distinguish how much is to be given to enthusiasm, and how much to reason . . . taking care . . . not to lose in terms of vague admiration, that solidity and truth of principle, upon which alone we can reason, and may be enabled to practise," Blake comments:

It is evident that Reynolds Wish'd none but Fools to be in the Arts & in order to this, he calls all others Vague Enthusiasts or Madmen.

What has Reasoning to do with the Art of Painting? [6]

His remarks on the eighth *Discourse* lay bare the empirical rationalism of some of Reynolds' theories:

Burke's Treatise on the Sublime & Beautiful is founded on the Opinion of Newton and Locke; on this Treatise Reynolds has grounded many of his assertions in all his Discourses. I read Burke's Treatise when very Young; at the same time I read Locke on Human Understanding & Bacon's Advancement of Learning; on Every one of these Books I wrote my Opinions & on looking them over find that my Notes on Reynolds in this Book are exactly Similar. I felt the same Contempt & Abhorrence then that I do now. They mock Inspiration & Vision. Inspiration and Vision was then, & now is, & I hope will always Remain, my Element, my Eternal Dwelling place; how can I then hear it Contemned without returning Scorn for Scorn? [7]

He even went so far in his romantic opposition to Reynolds' rationalism as to take issue with the latter's conception of the morality of artists as expressed in the following passage in the first *Discourse*: "When we read the lives of the most eminent Painters, every page informs us that no part of their time was spent in dissipation. . . ." Blake's withering reply is:

The lives of Painters say that Rafael Died of Dissipation. Idleness is one Thing & Dissipation Another. He who has Nothing to Dissipate Cannot Dissipate; the Weak Man may be Virtuous Enough, but will Never be an Artist.

Painters are noted for being Dissipated & Wild. [8]

It is a curious fact, and one not sufficiently accounted for, that the ideal classicism of the high Renaissance should form at least the

[6] *Ibid.,* p. 988. [7] *Ibid.,* p. 1011. [8] *Ibid.,* p. 982.

partial basis of the styles of two such otherwise different artists. Where Reynolds attempts romantically to color classic drawing, Blake dematerializes classic generalized forms under Gothic inspiration in order to give them romantic and mystic suggestiveness. In thus contrasting the styles of both men, we have a commentary on the various romantic potentialities of the classic which would bear more careful investigation than we can afford to give it here.

To return to Blake's particular development: he theoretically would have nothing to do with the imitation of nature in any form, whether realistic or ideal. To him the only reality was the imagination, which alone he considered inspired his compositions (a somewhat paradoxical thesis this, when his study of prints is remembered). This predominance of mind over matter, as it were, is explainable, of course, in his case on psychological—or should we say romantic?—grounds. The greater urgency of his mystical visions (and they grew in frequency and intensity with each passing year) over purely sensory or rational experience was enough to make him discount the importance of his reason or his senses. And he did so quite violently in his writings and conversations, if his everyday behavior appeared none the less ostensibly normal.

There were those, of course, who hearing him describe his visions and prejudices may have thought his mind unbalanced; there were certainly those who, bound by a traditional taste for academic representational art, considered his drawings the work of a lunatic. And after his death, down to the present, there has been a general feeling that at least he was not altogether sane by ordinary standards. It is significant, however, that none of his intimate friends thought him mad. They almost all comment rather on his striking appearance, particularly his large luminous eyes and, in general, the compelling quality of his personality.

These things must be said to prepare one for the tremendous impact felt on first meeting Blake's drawings done around 1795. One finds it in the well-known illustration to a scene in Act I of *Macbeth*, called *Pity* (Plate 26 a), described in the lines:

And pity, like a naked new-born babe,
Striding the blast, or heaven's cherubin, hors'd
Upon the sightless couriers of the air,
Shall blow the horrid deed in every eye.
That tears shall drown the wind.

Another example of the year 1795—a year in which he produced some of his most impressive designs—is *Elohim Creating Adam* (Plate 26 b). In its marvelous sweep of line and truly monumental force of conception it ranks with some of the greatest imaginative drawings of any time. Notable is the magical handling of light and shade, not for any naturalistic intent but purely as an emotive element in building up a profound and aweful effect. This *Creation of Adam* derives of course from that of Michelangelo on the Sistine Ceiling. But the latter, though sublime, is still an expression of emotion within a rational human frame, while Blake's picture seems to transcend all human barriers and pierce some mystical and ominous veil beyond reason altogether. *Hecate* (Plate 27 a) and *Death on the Pale Horse* have also this awe-inspiring quality.

Whereas the other-worldliness of these designs is of a terrible and foreboding order, the *Bathsheba at the Bath*, a tempera painting on canvas (a technique peculiar to Blake) has the quality of an idyllic dream, so balanced and relaxed are the rhythms of movement in the figure groups. And, likewise, in the ghostly, sonambulistic pace of *The Procession from Calvary* (Plate 27 b), in the National Gallery, London, painted about 1803, we have the supreme ecstatic expression of Blake's visions. It is effective beyond words to describe or any ordinary earth-bound style to represent.

We cannot discuss here the illustrated books of Blake—a neogothic practice, one may note, foreshadowing William Morris—with their combination of engraved text and color illuminations, a process which Blake invented himself. Like the involved series of prophetic books, whose meaning is so often obscure, the illustrations depend too much on an intimate knowledge of the text for any comprehensible exposition to be attempted in a general account such as this. One example of Blake's at times extraordinary decorative sense of the adjustment of text to illustration must suffice, a page from *Jerusalem* (Plate 28 a), where, as the text indicates, "the Divine hand found the two limits, Satan and Adam, in Albion's bosom."

Following the books of the 1780's and '90's the next important work Blake did in the way of color drawings is the set of illustrations for Milton's *Paradise Lost*, done in 1808, of which we have already mentioned the *Creation of Eve*. In the somewhat earlier *She Shall Be Called Woman* (Plate 29 a), in the Metropolitan Museum, we get the weaker side of Blake's imagery, however, where in fact it comes close to a rather fatuous sentimentality. He was not always able to keep his work, then, at the high level of expression one finds in the drawings and tempera paintings of 1795 to 1803. Between 1803 and 1818, furthermore, he suffered poverty and neglect and this may explain the falling off of much of his work in force and imaginative fervor. He was also a tremendously prolific worker and probably his dreams, as it were, ran thin. Fortunately, from 1800 on until his death he was patronized by two loyal friends, a Mr. Butts at first and later, from 1818 to 1827, by the artist John Linnell. Butts is known above all to collectors for having commissioned in 1822 the famous series of watercolor drawings illustrating the Book of Job, now in The Pierpont Morgan Library, New York. Some of these are generally conceded to be Blake's masterpieces in point of imaginative range and grandeur of conception. In a single earlier design, *Satan Smiting Job with Boils* (Plate 28 b), tempera on mahogany panel, another curious Blake technique, we have a splendid prototype to one of the greatest of the Morgan series. There is nothing to equal the magnificent terror of this in all the artist's work.

The Job drawings occupied him for a number of years and he finally made a set of engravings after them. The crowning work of his last years, however, and the work which he left unfinished at his death, is the series of illustrations to Dante's *Divine Comedy*, many of which are in the Tate Gallery, London. Here, in perhaps the greatest and most extensive allegorical poem ever written, Blake found the full measure of his powers. In sixty-eight drawings for the *Inferno*, twenty for the *Purgatorio*, and ten for the *Paradiso* he illumined Dante's medieval panorama of the progress of a soul from hell to heaven as it had not been done since Botticelli. In one of the most telling of the scenes from the *Purgatorio—Dante and Virgil Ascending the Mountain* (Plate 29 b)—Virgil rests high up on the rocks and waits for Dante who climbs below. A dark cloud crosses in a circle before the sun. The sea is dark, lit with yellow at the horizon. In its great architectonic simplicity and, more than anything else, its magnificent suggestive washes of color—the effect is somewhat lost in black and white—this is a fitting climax to the imaginative heights to which Blake showed himself more than once capable of rising.

To conclude: In some of his best designs Blake is certainly in a class with the greatest imaginative artists of all time. It is true his technical equipment was often faulty. His numerous technical processes—adapted or invented—are indications, in a sense, of some uncertainty in respect to mere execution, although at the same time they often reflect the inevitable struggle with material means of representation which all great artists, and none less than Picasso in our own day, have experienced in a search for a more complete externalization of their visions. Let us say simply that Blake was touched by a fire which generated images he was sometimes able to control, giving limit and extension to them in the best of his designs; while at other times he lost his grip upon this super-real world and came dangerously near to a complete cleavage with the ordinary bounds of sanity, just as Dali today has forced Surrealism in the same direction.

The explanation of Blake's states of mind are perhaps better left to the psychiatrist. He might say, for example, that Blake's mania for line is a common symptom of schizophrenia, from which Van Gogh and other imaginative artists of a very high order are said to have suffered. Whatever the cause, the art of both Blake and Van Gogh has at least moved many of the so-called sane to genuine wonder and excitement. It may be that in the final analysis Blake, Van Gogh, and artists of their kind, dwell in a world of a higher sanity from which we of a more humdrum, normal, temperament are all but excluded.

CHAPTER V

JOSEPH M. W. TURNER AND JOHN CONSTABLE

If Reynolds is an English institution, Turner is a legend. Ruskin, who did so much to fashion the Turner myth, considered his hero the greatest landscape painter who ever lived. We may have outgrown, or perhaps only outlived, the spell of the Victorian critic-seer, but it is still difficult for us to look upon Turner clearly and as a whole. He was so prolific, so incredibly energetic, so various, it is not surprising that when praising him we cannot be certain that we have not been carried away by the trickery of a super-mountebank; or that when criticizing him we cannot be certain that the canvas under criticism is truly typical and deserving of other than isolated censure. This confusion of impression has led some cautious critics to place the artist in a sort of eccentric category. In this way he has been accepted or dismissed without disturbing too much the broad pattern of art history. Fortunately, perhaps, we have not the space in which to weigh the detailed evidence pro and con. We must be, therefore, to a degree dogmatic.

From our point of view, then, Turner is a reactionary painter, however confusing and, in some ways contradictory are the many facets of his artistic personality. There is the Turner who emulated Claude, giving that master's picturesque prospect an, at times, absurd expansiveness and bringing it thereby to a ridiculous conclusion as a landscape form. There is the Turner who copied and attempted to out-do the Dutch seascapists. And there is the Turner, too rarely in evidence, who forgot past painters for a moment and permitted himself to be moved directly by a particular scene; who did not seek to use this scene simply as a point of picturesque departure but rather accepted it as the primary stuff out of which, and controlled by which, he created his painting. But the Turner we know throughout most of his career is a compound of the first two: the great showman, the eclectic, the Reynolds of landscape painting—more impressive on first acquaintance than he really is.

Set off against Hogarth, Gainsborough, and Blake, all of them more or less independent and "contemporary" artists, in a sense which promised much for the future vitality of English painting, Reynolds and Turner stand out as would-be leaders who offered a compromise between a fashionable neo-classical idealism in subject matter and a particularized or naturalistic treatment of light and color. In both painters the uncertain balance between these opposing points of view resulted, more often than not, in a sterile kind of art (for the future, at any rate), which, given the "official" acceptance of their work, had serious consequences. Their spectacular pictorial sophistication, based alas on none too mature imaginations, is a forerunner of the bathos of Victorian art.

Born in London in 1775, Turner may have worked at the age of eleven for a floral painter. At thirteen he attended a drawing school at Margate and studied under Thomas Malton, an architectural draftsman of considerable ability and discipline. From this training the young Turner went on to coloring prints for J. R. Smith, the engraver, and to washing in backgrounds for architects' drawings. In 1789 he entered the Royal Academy schools and won his first success in exhibition as a landscape watercolorist. Ten years later his work was sufficiently valued by the critics to make possible his election as an Associate of the Royal Academy and in 1802 he became a full R. A., an astonishingly rapid climb of the official ladder of recognition. In this same year he travelled through France and Switzerland to Strassburg. Between 1807 and 1819 he superintended the engraving of his *Liber Studiorum*, a collection of types of landscape composition in emulation of, and in competition with, Claude's famous *Liber Veritatis*. He visited Belgium, Holland, and the Rhine in 1817. In 1818 he was in Scotland and in 1819 he first visited Italy. From 1833 to 1835 he spent increasingly longer periods abroad, particularly in Venice, North Italy, and Switzerland. In 1850 he exhibited for the last time and died the following year.

[49]

The geographical range of his landscape interests should be noted first of all. It represents an extension of a particular kind of native topographical painting with which Turner first came in contact under Malton: a careful pictorial documentation of notable country houses, churches, and towns, for which there was an increasing demand in the second half of the eighteenth century. This type of picture was sponsored by three groups of patrons: by antiquarians interested in Gothic architectural remains; by proud owners who desired a pictorial record of their country estates to set beside portraits of their persons; and by the general public seeking vicarious travel, either to places it had never seen or in retrospect to those it had previously visited. This documentation of place merges with Turner into the picturesque view, with all its superimposed " effects "—suggestive limitlessness of prospect, semi-classical reminiscences of history painting, and related literary associations. An early and good example is the *Kirkstall Abbey* (Plate 30 a). The all-inclusive, cumulative reference of such a medley of landscape interests explains, of course, Turner's immediate popularity with both critics and public from the very beginning of his career. He appealed to both sophisticated and popular tastes. Such wide approbation, one feels, is surely traceable to a conscious or unconscious genius for display, and it is this characteristic which in Turner is developed to a high point as time goes on.

For reasons suggested in the above it is difficult to treat his art in terms of any systematic stylistic progression. Because of the unpredictable nature of his eclecticism it is almost impossible to separate his relatively original landscapes from those directly inspired by some past master. One can only outline, therefore, very broadly the main periods of his work where now one, now another, influence is uppermost. From 1790 to about 1797 we have the architectural and topographical views in watercolor mentioned above. From about 1797 to about 1805 date his first oil paintings, his assimilation of the influence of his English contemporary Girtin, and his early attempts to emulate Poussin and the Dutch. From 1805 to 1829 marks a long middle period of mixed challenges of past masters, particularly Van Goyen, William van de Velde the Younger, Cuyp, Hobbema, Ruysdael, and above all Claude. His admiration for the latter painter he memorialized in a famous gift to the National Gallery, London. As outlined in his will, he stipulated that, if accepted by the Gallery, his *Sun Rising Through Vapor* and *Dido Building Carthage* (Plate 30 c) should hang near two Claude landscapes. This request was carried out, and the above canvases now hang side by side with Claude's *Marriage of Isaac and Rebecca* and *Embarkation of the Queen of Sheba*. The appropriateness of the second picture as a partner for the *Dido* is obvious. The composition in both is much the same. The style of architecture is similar, as is the expanse of sun-lit sea stretching to a far horizon. Turner's contribution is to magnify the older master's every effect: a more majestic scale of building, a more extensive sea, a blaze of sun in place of a cool clear light. The restrained quiet of the Claudian mood has been shattered by a generous application of heat, as it were, to every part of the older picture. In a different fashion, but with a like exaggeration of the original, *The Ship Wreck* (Plate 30 b), painted in 1805, outdoes the Dutch on their own sea, so to speak. With perhaps Van de Velde or Van Goyen as starting points, Turner lets loose a storm which no factual-minded Dutchman would have dared to represent. Had he by chance been exposed to such a catastrophic deluge, one feels, he would never have lived to paint it.

During these years of imitative display, however, there is a rare sub-period when Turner produced some landscapes whose basis is direct experience of an actual scene with little or no compositional inspiration from some master of the past. *A Frosty Morning; Sunrise* (Plate 31 c) is the masterpiece of this kind in its quiet undramatic treatment of a truly English scene. It comes as a cool refreshing note in the midst of a long chorus of emulative thunderings.

But the melodramatic was in Turner's blood, and after about 1829 he submits to few restraints upon his excited imagination. His romanticism is now at full flood and in the last twenty years of his life he produces canvases which, depending upon one's partisanship, spell either genius of the highest order or suspiciously enigmatic posturing which bodes ill for the future. During these years the break takes place with whatever is premeditated or prearranged in the Claude tradition, whatever is naturalistic in the Dutch, in favor of pyrotechnical displays for their own sake or for pictures overloaded with detail. In the first class is the well-known *Rain, Steam and Speed; The Great Western Railway* (Plate 31 a). Impressive on first sight, as any display of fireworks inevitably is, one's confidence in the artist's sense of dramatic fitness is somewhat shaken when one discovers that as a symbol of speed he has introduced a hare running before the engine. It is perhaps a small point at which to jib, in an otherwise grand conception of mechanical and elemental energy, but here, nevertheless, is surely an ominous symptom of that instability of imagination which is a direct cause of Victorian triviality of sentiment.

Of the second class of picture Ruskin has this significant comment to make: Turner, he says,

looked for litter like Covent Garden Wreck after the Market. His pictures are often full of it from side to side. Their foregrounds differ from all others in the natural way that things have of lying about in them. Even his richest vegetation in ideal work is confused; and he delights in shingle, débris, and heaps of fallen stones. The last words he ever spoke to me about a picture were in a gentle exaltation about his St. Gothard: ' that litter of stones which I endeavoured to represent.' [1]

The good Victorian is here admiring, not criticizing, " litter " and he seems to take for granted that it is rather an original feature in Turner's work. He overlooks the fact that the painter gets some of his love of litter from the old picturesque-classical tradition. Therein heaps of fallen stones, ruined houses and mills, tangled foliage, ragged clothing, were all used as sentimental symbols of the passing of time—marks of the here-and-nowness of a fake realism. But picturesque artists like Gaspard Poussin, Salvator Rosa, Pater, Boucher, and Moreland do keep these symbols under a certain control; their litter has a certain orderliness about

[1] *Modern Painters,* vol. V, chap. 9.

it. Not so Turner: in *A Regatta at Cowes* (Plate 31 b), for example, he piles on litter for litter's sake, so to speak, and the limitless cornucopia of detail would be almost unbearably chaotic were it not for the veil of light which he draws over the whole. (In like manner Monet and other Impressionists provide, at times, a superficial unity to their documents of actuality and from this standpoint, and this one only, Turner is their progenitor.)

Simplicity and clarity of effect, then, are not Turner's strong points. As he grew older his penchant was for a sort of massive, Byronic discursiveness. (He was, of course, an admirer of the poet.) That this boisterous passion for crowding sea-pieces with breaking waves, floating spars, and all the gear of boats bordered sometimes on the ridiculous, was recognized by W. M. Thackeray, who characteristically did not share Ruskin's passion for the trivial. In describing *The Slave Ship* (Plate 32 a), now in the Museum of Fine Arts, Boston, he writes:

Rocks of gamboge are marked down upon the canvas; flakes of white laid on with a trowel; bladders of vermilion madly spirted here and there. Yonder is the slaver rocking in the midst of a flashing foam of white-lead. The sun glares down upon a horrible sea of emerald and purple, into which chocolate-coloured slaves are plunged, and chains that will not sink; and round these are floundering such a race of fishes as never was seen since the saeculum Pyrrhae; gasping dolphins redder than the reddest herrings; horrid spreading polypi, like huge, slimy, poached eggs, in which hapless niggers, plunge and disappear. Ye gods, what a ' middle passage '! [2]

This tract against slavery is, by the way, an interesting fore-runner of the sensational moral anecdote which is a characteristic of Victorian painting. That Thackeray did not like it is no proof that he disliked on general grounds any exaggerated emotional treatment of a subject. He may simply not have been a con-vinced anti-slaver. Melodrama in itself, at any rate, did not keep him from admiring *The Fighting Téméraire* (Plate 32 b), wherein Turner symbolizes the British pride in a ship of the fleet which helped to defeat Napoleon at Trafalgar. Thackeray describes the

[2] Quoted by A. J. Finberg in his *Life of J. M. W. Turner* (Oxford University Press, 1939), p. 378.

scene, in a prose as unrestrained as the lighting of the picture, as follows:

The old Téméraire is dragged to her last home by a little, spiteful, diabolical steamer. A mighty red sun, amidst a host of flaring clouds, sinks to rest on one side of the picture, and illumines a river that seems interminable, and a countless navy that fades away into such a wonderful distance as never was painted before. The little demon of a steamer is belching out a volume (why do I say a volume? not a hundred volumes could express it) of foul, lurid, red-hot, malignant smoke, paddling furiously and lashing up the water round about it; while behind it (a cold grey moon looking down on it), slow, sad, and majestic, follows the brave old ship, with death, as it were, written on her. . . .[3]

The novelist's enthusiasm here reveals the secret of Turner's chief appeal to his public, both intellectual and popular. He had an instinct for the kind of programmatic subject interest which had to be incorporated into landscape painting to raise it, in the estimation of a traditional history-loving connoisseur, above the vulgarity of a simple documentation of raw nature. He sensed also that to appeal to the less knowing he had to avoid a landscape which demands for its appreciation a careful concentration upon values of color and formal relationships. Such values are not immediately perceptible to the casual observer, and few can afford to wait until they recognize them.

In Constable we have an artist who was incapable of larding his pictures with " subject " interest. He had none of Turner's showmanship and thus he never felt the need to post over the length and breadth of England, Scotland, and the Continent for " views " to tickle the traveler's, or would-be traveler's, taste. He denied himself, as a consequence, a fashionable and popular following all his life. That he might better understand what he was painting he rigidly restricted himself to the English scene, and therein to only a few parts of it, most of them encompassed by the Stour district in Suffolkshire, the country in and about Salisbury, the Channel coast, and Hampstead Heath on the outskirts of London.[4] In many ways he is the prototype of Cézanne:

[3] Finberg, op. cit., p. 373.
[4] As a young man he attempted to paint the romantically picturesque, and, there-

in stubborn singleness of purpose; limited geographical range of landscape interest; freshness and profundity of examination of light in relation to color and atmosphere in relation to space; and determined searching after technical means to "realize" observations on canvas. In this passion for the investigation of certain aspects of the world about him, Constable had more in common with contemporary scientists like Davy and Faraday than he had with his convention-bound fellow artists.

The son of a well-to-do ,miller, he was born in East Bergholt, Suffolkshire, in 1776, one year after Turner. Largely self-taught, he was a rather uncomfortable, probably secretly resentful, student at the Royal Academy schools in 1799. Slow in developing his powers compared with Turner, he was only beginning to exhibit his landscapes publicly around the turn of the century. Thereafter, like Cézanne, he longed all his life for "official" recognition, and gained what little he did only after years of effort. Unlike Cézanne, however, he was not a conscious, or perhaps we should say determined, revolutionary. He was unromantically "respectable" in his everyday life. Almost always independent of patronage from a financial standpoint, he was on good terms with the Tory government of the day and the chief politician of the Academy, Joseph Farrington. Nevertheless, he found it so difficult to alter his personal landscape style to suit the official taste, however much he tried, that it was not until 1819—twenty years after Turner—that he was made an A. R. A. He had to wait another ten years—twenty-seven after Turner—before he was elected R. A., an honor which did him little good, financially or otherwise, for he only lived eight years more, until 1837, to "enjoy" it.

How did he stand in relation to the old masters? In contrast to Turner and Reynolds, he sought to assimilate, not emulate their works. Unlike academic worshippers of a past golden age, he never underrated his own day and his own powers as an artist. He was out to contribute to the past, so to speak, not to live off it.

fore, fashionable mountains of the Lake District but he was apparently not moved by such scenery and did not return to it.

He paid genuine tribute to such landscape masters as Claude, the Poussins, Rubens, Hobbema, Ruysdael, Wilson, and Gainsborough. His *Country Lane* (Plate 33 a), for example, in the National Gallery, London, undoubtedly owes something to Hobbema and Gainsborough. But it is not a servile or ostentatious copy. He clarifies and integrates these painters' compositions to a point where all nature—air, light, tree, and field—takes on an extraordinary vividness and sense of unification. His brushwork is more broken than theirs, his colors more primary and "direct" in application, the better to explain, as Rubens had suggested earlier, the vibrant quality of light refraction through moisture-laden air. Likewise, his *Weymouth Bay* (Plate 33 b), recalling as it does the seascapes of Jakob van Ruysdael, presents by comparison a so much more intensified and supremely naturalistic vision that no thought of plagiarism can enter one's mind. So soo, *The Salt Box* (Plate 34 a), in its subtle coördination of all the elements in a landscape, transforms the more pedestrian Dutch description of natural phenomena into a vital and masterly unity. And his *Malvern Hall* (Plate 34 c), inspired no doubt by Richard Wilson and eventually, through him, by Claude, is nevertheless a magnificently personal re-statement of those qualities of naturalistic light and air which had been originally a part of a now moribund picturesque tradition. In short, while Constable undoubtedly learned much from older painters in the architecture of picture making, while he studied carefully their naturalistic observations, and even their picturesque inventions, he never felt any compunction to compete with these masters in order, like Turner, to buttress a shaky ego.

On the contrary, he points to the practice of past masters to vindicate his own independence of them. "What," he says, "were the habits of Claude and the Poussins? Though surrounded with palaces filled with pictures, they made the fields their chief places of study." [5] And of himself, he says (so afraid was he of forming the academic habit of breeding new pictures from old): "When

[5] C. R. Leslie's *Memoirs of the Life of John Constable* [revised and edited by the Hon. Andrew Shirley] (London: The Medici Society, 1937), p. 362.

I sit down to make a sketch from nature, the first thing I try to do is, *to forget that I have ever seen a picture*." [6] At the end of his life, in 1836, when presumably he had nothing to fear from speaking out (he had an acid tongue at all times, which may be the reason why he was not earlier elected a member of the Academy [7]) he discusses at greater length the whole question of reviving the past. When we remember that the fashion of style revivals proved to be the greatest curse of English 19th century art we can appreciate his foresight, and how much he spoke against the grain, when he said:

The attempt to revive styles that have existed in former ages may for a time appear to be successful, but experience may now surely teach us its impossibility. I might put on a suit of Claude Lorraine's clothes and walk into the street, and the many who know Claude but slightly would pull off their hats to me, but I should at last meet with someone more intimately acquainted with him, who would expose me to the contempt I merited.

It is thus in all the fine arts. A new Gothic building, or a new missal, is in reality little less absurd than a *new ruin*. The Gothic architecture, sculpture, and painting belong to peculiar ages. The feelings that guided their inventors are unknown to us, we contemplate them with associations, many of which, however vague and dim, have a strong hold on our imaginations, and we feel indignant at the attempt to cheat us by any modern mimicry of their peculiarities.

[6] *Memoirs,* pp. 366-367.

[7] According to Leslie, " In some points of Constable's character a striking resemblance may be traced to that of Hogarth. Though their walks of art were wide apart, yet each formed a style more truly original than that of any of his contemporaries, and this, in part, prevented each from enjoying the fame to which he was entitled. They both incurred the imputation of vanity, perhaps from much vainer men, because they vindicated their own merits.—Hogarth expressed in a witty etching (*The Battle of the Pictures*) his sense of the injustice he suffered from the connoisseurs, and Constable spoke his opinions openly of the critics; and with point, truth, and freedom, as did Hogarth, of contemporary artists, and each by so doing made bitter enemies.—In conclusion, they were both genuine Englishmen; warmly attached to the character and institutions of their country; alike quick in detecting cant and quackery, not only in religion and politics, but in taste and in the arts; and though they sometimes may have carried the prejudices of their John Bullism too far, they each deserved well of their country, as steady opponents to the influence of foreign vice, folly, and bad taste; in which, however, Hogarth's class of subjects enabled him to exert himself with far the most effect." (*Memoirs,* pp. 357-358).

It is to be lamented that the tendency of taste is at present too much towards this kind of imitation, which, as long as it lasts, can only act as a blight on art, by engaging talents that might have stamped the Age with a character of its own, in the vain endeavour to reanimate deceased Art, in which the utmost that can be accomplished will be to reproduce a body without a soul.[8]

We have said that Constable had more in common with the natural scientists of his day than he had with his fellow artists. " When young," he tells us (November 10, 1835), " I was extremely fond of reading poetry, and also fond of music, and I played myself a little; but as I advanced in life and in art, I soon gave up the latter; and now after thirty years, I must say that the sister arts have less hold on my mind in its occasional ramblings from my one pursuit than the sciences, especially the study of geology, which more than any other, seems to satisfy my mind." [9] He must have been flattered, then, when Faraday expressed admiration for his lectures on " The History of Landscape Painting," given at the Royal Institution in 1836. Unfortunately, we know nothing more of this suggestive meeting. On the other hand, Leslie assures us of the intimate friendship that existed between Constable and the chemist George Field (1777?-1854), whose *Chromatography; or a treatise on Colours and Pigments, and of their Powers in Painting* was published in 1835. Field was not only an expert in the chemistry of pigments, but he also made some investigation of the relation of light to color (perhaps with Constable's assistance and certainly with his knowledge), and invented, among other things, conical lenses " which produced a continuous rainbow with varied effects of refraction." [10] In the *Chromotography* he speaks of the luminosity of shadows, and he points to the error made by many artists who regarded " shadows only as darkness, blackness, or the mere absence of light, when in truth shadows are infinitely varied by colour." [11] That Constable had made no such mistake his paintings bear profound

[8] *Memoirs*, pp. 404-405.
[9] *Memoirs*, pp. 360-361.
[10] *Dictionary of National Biography*, vol. VI, p. 1269.
[11] Quoted by Leslie, *Memoirs*, p. 398, footnote.

witness. They may well, in fact, have directed Field's attention to the phenomenon in question. However that may be, what is even more significant in the light of Constable's interest in the sciences are some of his remarks on painting. " In such an age as this," he once insisted, " painting should be *understood*, not looked on with blind wonder, nor considered only as a poetic aspiration, but as a pursuit, *legitimate*, *scientific*, and *mechanical*." [12] In the same vein he concluded his last lecture on " The History of Landscape Painting ":

As your kind attention has so long been given to my description of pictures, it may now be well to consider in what estimation we are to hold them, and in what class we are to place the men who have produced them.—It appears to me that pictures have been over-valued; held up by a blind admiration as ideal things, and almost as standards by which nature is to be judged rather than the reverse; and this false estimate has been sanctioned by the extravagant epithets that have ben applied to painters, as ' the divine,' ' the inspired,' and so forth. Yet, in reality, what are the most sublime productions of the pencil but selections of some of the forms of nature, and copies of a few of her evanescent effects; and this is the result, not of inspiration, but of long and patient study, under the direction of much good sense.—It was said by Sir Thomas Lawrence, that ' we can never hope to compete with nature in the beauty and delicacy of her separate forms or colours,—our only chance lies in selection and combination.' Nothing can be more true,—and it may be added, that selection and combination are learned from nature herself, who constantly presents us with compositions of her own, far more beautiful than the happiest arranged by human skill. I have endeavoured to draw a line between genuine art and mannerism, but even the greatest painters have never been wholly untainted by manner.—Painting is a science, and should be pursued as an inquiry into the laws of nature. Why, then, may not landscape painting be considered as a branch of natural philosophy, of which pictures are but the experiments? [13]

Startling though such statements are (foreshadowing as they do something of the pseudo-scientific attitude of the French Impressionists) they must be considered, however, with reference to the incestuous, inbred academic painting of his day, to which he was violently opposed and whose admirers, furthermore, had con-

[12] *Memoirs*, p. 361.   [13] *Memoirs*, pp. 402-403.

sistently avoided his art. With this in mind we can perhaps discount his somewhat exaggerated respect for what appeared to him to be the scientist's greater claims to originality in the observation of nature; and his understandable wish to associate himself with the discovery-making potential of the latter's occupation. He must also have been aware, if only subconsciously, that his kinship with men of research in fields other than painting, and the interests he shared with them, recalled more forcibly than did the preoccupations of conservative academicians the glibly praised Renaissance, when, as with Leonardo, it was possible for the artist and the scientist to be united in one person, or at least for the one to make free use of the other's discoveries.

But however much Constable in theory may have wished to make of painting a servant of science, his own work on the whole is a suffiicent denial of the kind of photographic documentation of actual appearances which such a role might imply. It is only when he tightened up and smoothed out the paint surface of his canvases in a mistaken attempt to mollify the academic critics who accused him of lack of training that he became labored and mechanical. Such a charge may be leveled against his *Dedham Mill* in the Taft Museum, Cincinnati (Plate 34 b). But compare the Victoria and Albert Museum version of the famous *Hay Wain* (Plate 35 a), which he painted for himself, with the version in the London National Gallery (Plate 35 b), "finished" for public consumption. Here we can see at once the difference between a selective distillation of natural phenomena for artistic purposes and the same material slicked-up and devitalized to give a spuriously vivid impression of actuality. That the doctoring has been only skin deep in the "finished" picture is fortunate. The essential Constable is there for the perceptive eye to discover. How else can we explain the revolutionary effect of the picture on Delacroix when he saw it in the *Salon* of 1824? That Constable was never bound by the actual appearance of things we have evidence in his *Memoirs*.[14] But no such reassurance is needed to

[14] In 1840 Leslie and a Mr. Purton visited the scenes of many of Constable's pictures in Suffolkshire. They found that while some of his canvases were start-

convince us of the passionate recreative artistry in *On the River Stour* (Plate 33 c). This magnificent ode to the earth and sky, light, air, and water, fuses the primary substance of a world into a universal combination and brings it miraculously within the confines of a picture frame.

And here we shall conclude with a final comparison of Turner's and Constable's handling of a scene whose central motive is the same, Salisbury Cathedral. In the one (Plate 36 b) we have the over-ripe product of a picturesque classicism, Byronic in its glittering expansiveness; in the other (Plate 36 a) we have in pictorial translation the Wordsworth-like " speech of common men," the independent observation and expression of which has been in effect the subject of these lectures. Begun by Hogarth, sensitively explored by Gainsborough, explosively sponsored by Blake, the English individualistic current in all its satirical, mystical, and naturalistic variety here comes to an end, so far as painting is concerned, for many a long year. It remained for Delacroix, Courbet, Manet, and Cézanne, and the host of their fellows, to take up the challenge and bring some of the things that Englishmen had begun to a splendid fruition.

ling in their " resemblance " to the original scenes, of others they found that Constable " had rather combined and varied the materials, than given exact views. In the larger compositions, such as *The White Horse* and *The Hay Wain,* both from this neighbourhood, he has increased the width of the river to great advantage; and wherever there was an opportunity, he was fond of introducing the tower of Dedham Church, which is seen from many points near Flatford. . . . The appearance of Dedham mill is greatly improved in every picture Constable painted of it, by his showing the water-wheel, which in reality is hidden." (*Memoirs,* p. 372).

PLATES

PLATE 1

b) HOGARTH, Frederick Frankland (*ca.* 1730).
Courtesy of the Henry E. Huntington
Library and Art Gallery, San Marino, California.

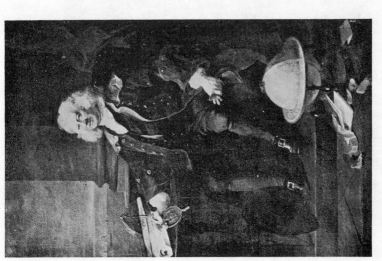

a) HOGARTH, Captain Coram (1739).
Foundling Hospital, London.

PLATE 2

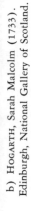

b) HOGARTH, Sarah Malcolm (1733).
Edinburgh, National Gallery of Scotland.

a) HOGARTH, William James (1744).

Collection of the
Worcester Art Museum, Mass.

PLATE 3

b) HOGARTH, The Dance (*ca.* 1753?: Sketch for "Analysis of Beauty").
South London Art Gallery.

a) HOGARTH, Simon Fraser, Lord Lovat (1746).
Engraving after picture in National Portrait Gallery, London.

PLATE 4

a) HOGARTH, A Family Group.
London, National Gallery.

b) HOGARTH, Committee of House of Commons examining Bambridge (1729).
Engraving after picture in National Portrait Gallery, London.

PLATE 5

a) HOGARTH, Wedding of Stephen Beckingham
and Mary Cox (1729).

*Courtesy of the
Metropolitan Museum of Art.*

b) HOGARTH, Scene from Gay's "Beggar's Opera" (1728).
London, Tate Gallery.

PLATE 6

a) HOGARTH, Scene from Dryden's "Indian Emperor" (1731).
London, Lord Ilchester Collection.

b) HOGARTH, Gin Lane (1751).

Engraving.

c) HOGARTH, Beer Street (1751).

Engraving.

PLATE 7

a) HOGARTH, Marriage à la Mode, " The Contract " (1745).
London, Tate Gallery.

b) HOGARTH, Marriage à la Mode, " The Toilet Scene " (1745).
London, Tate Gallery.

PLATE 8

a) HOGARTH, Taste in High Life (1742).

Engraving.

b) HOGARTH, Miss Mary Edwards (*ca.* 1742).

Copyright, The Frick Collection, New York.

PLATE 9

a) REYNOLDS, Parody of Raphael's "School of Athens" (1751).
Dublin, National Gallery of Ireland.

b) REYNOLDS, Lady Betty Hamilton
(1758).
Joseph E. Widener Collection,
Elkins Park, Pa.

c) REYNOLDS, Nelly O'Brien
(ca. 1762).
London, Wallace Collection.

PLATE 10

a) REYNOLDS, Mrs. Billington (1790).
Courtesy of the New York Public Library.

b) REYNOLDS, Lady Sarah Bunbury
Sacrificing to the Graces (1765).
Courtesy of the Art Institute, Chicago.

c) REYNOLDS, Miss Frances Crewe
(1775?).
Marquess of Crewe, London.

d) REYNOLDS, Master Crewe as
King Henry VIII (1776).
Marquess of Crewe, London.

PLATE 11

a) REYNOLDS, The Graces Adorning a Term of Hymen
(The daughters of Sir William Montgomery: 1774).
London, National Gallery.

b) POUSSIN, Bacchanalian Dance.
London, National Gallery.

PLATE 12

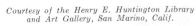

a) REYNOLDS, Mrs. Siddons as
" The Tragic Muse " (1784).

*Courtesy of the Henry E. Huntington Library
and Art Gallery, San Marino, Calif.*

b) MICHELANGELO, Isaiah.
Sistine Ceiling.

c) REYNOLDS, Jane, Countess of
Harrington (1777-79).

*Courtesy of the Henry E. Huntington Library
and Art Gallery, San Marino, Calif.*

PLATE 13

b) REYNOLDS, Oliver Goldsmith (1770).
British Museum (Dwg. for portrait in
Duke of Bedford's Collection, Woburn Abbey).

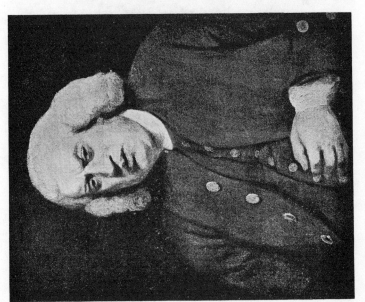

a) REYNOLDS, Dr. Samuel Johnson (1772).
London, National Gallery.

PLATE 14

a) REYNOLDS, Self-Portrait (1775).
Florence, Uffizi.

b) REYNOLDS, Lord Heathfield (1788).
London, National Gallery.

c) REYNOLDS, Death of Cardinal Beaufort (1789).
Engr. after picture in Lord Leconfield's Collection.

PLATE 15

a) GAINSBOROUGH, Cornard Wood (1748).
London, National Gallery.

b) HOBBEMA, The Holford Landscape.

Courtesy National Gallery of Art, Washington.

PLATE 16

a) GAINSBOROUGH, Mr. and Mrs. Andrews (*ca.* 1755-59).
G. W. Andrews Collection, England.

b) HAYMAN, Children of Jonathan Tyers.
Mrs. Derek Fitzgerald Collection, England.

PLATE 17

a) GAINSBOROUGH, Lady Innes (*ca.* 1757).

Copyright, The Frick Collection, New York.

b) GAINSBOROUGH, The Painter's Daughters (*ca.* 1757-58). London, National Gallery.

PLATE 18

b) GAINSBOROUGH, Benjamin Truman (*ca.* 1770).
The Brewery, Spitalfields.

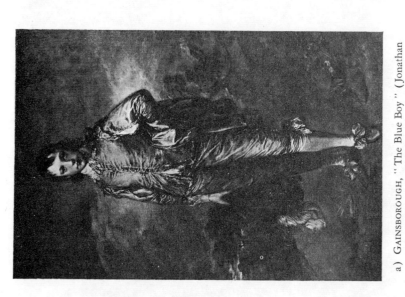

a) GAINSBOROUGH, "The Blue Boy" (Jonathan
Buttall, *ca.* 1769).

*Courtesy of the Henry E. Huntington Library and
Art Gallery, San Marino, California.*

PLATE 19

b) GAINSBOROUGH, The Honorable Frances Duncombe (*ca.* 1777-78).

Copyright, The Frick Collection, New York.

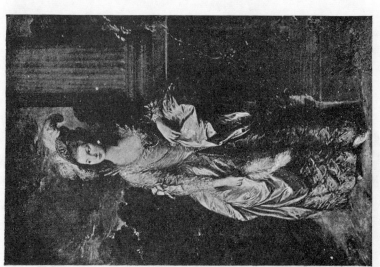

a) GAINSBOROUGH, Mrs. Graham (1777). Edinburgh, National Gallery of Scotland.

PLATE 20

a) GAINSBOROUGH, Sketch for a Landscape (*ca.* 1780).
H. Horne Collection, England.

b) GAINSBOROUGH, The Bridge (*ca.* 1777).
London, National Gallery.

PLATE 21

b) GAINSBOROUGH, Mrs. Siddons (1785).
London, National Gallery.

a) GAINSBOROUGH, Rustic Children.
London, National Gallery.

PLATE 22

b) GAINSBOROUGH, The Mall in St. James's Park (*ca.* 1784).

Copyright, The Frick Collection, New York.

a) GAINSBOROUGH, "The Morning Walk" (Squire Hallett and His Wife: 1785). London, Lord Rothschild Collection.

PLATE 23

a) BLAKE, Creation of Eve (1808).
Courtesy of the Museum of Fine Arts, Boston.
Watercolor.

b) MICHELANGELO, Creation of Eve.
Sistine Ceiling.

PLATE 24

a) BLAKE, The Wise and Foolish Virgins (*ca.* 1822).
Courtesy of the Metropolitan Museum of Art.
Watercolor.

b) ANGEL, Westminster Abbey, triforium,
south transept (13th century).

PLATE 25

a) BLAKE, Penance of Jane Shore (*ca.* 1780).
Graham Robertson Collection, England.

Drawing.

b) BLAKE, Oberon and Titania asleep on a
Lily Petal (*ca.* 1795). From
" Song of Los."
London, British Museum.

Watercolor.

PLATE 26

a) BLAKE, Pity (from "Macbeth," 1795).
Graham Robertson Collection, England.

Watercolor.

b) BLAKE, Elohim Creating Adam (1795).
Graham Robertson Collection, England.

Watercolor.

PLATE 27

a) BLAKE, Hecate (1806).
Graham Robertson Collection, England.

Color print.

b) BLAKE, Procession from Calvary (*ca.* 1803).
London, National Gallery.

Tempera on paper.

PLATE 28

a) BLAKE, Page from " Jerusalem " (1818).
London, British Museum.

Engraving.

b) BLAKE, Satan Smiting Job with Boils.
London, Tate Gallery.

Tempera, on mahogany panel.

PLATE 29

b) BLAKE, Dante and Virgil Ascending the Mountain (from the "Divine Comedy": *ca.* 1827). London, Tate Gallery.
Watercolor.

a) BLAKE, She Shall Be Called Woman (1807).
Courtesy of the Metropolitan Museum of Art.
Watercolor.

PLATE 30

a) TURNER, Kirkstall Abbey, Yorkshire (before 1800).
Fitzwilliam Museum, Cambridge. *Watercolor.*

b) TURNER, The Shipwreck (1805).
National Gallery, London.

c) TURNER, Dido Building Carthage (1815).
National Gallery, London.

a) TURNER, Rain, Steam and Speed (1844).
National Gallery, London.

b) TURNER, A Regatta at Cowes (1827).
Tate Gallery, London.

c) TURNER, A Frosty Morning (1813).
National Gallery, London.

PLATE 32

a) TURNER, The Slave Ship (1840).

Courtesy of Museum of Fine Arts, Boston.

b) TURNER, The Fighting Téméraire (1838).
Tate Gallery, London.

PLATE 33

b) CONSTABLE, Weymouth Bay (*ca.* 1816).
National Gallery, London.

c) CONSTABLE, On the River Stour.
*Courtesy of the Phillips Memorial Gallery,
Washington, D. C.*

a) CONSTABLE, A Country Lane (*ca.* 1826).
National Gallery, London.

b) CONSTABLE, Dedham Mill (*ca.* 1820).

*Courtesy of the Taft Museum,
Cincinnati.*

a) CONSTABLE, The Salt Box, Hampstead Heath (1821(?)).
National Gallery, London.

c) CONSTABLE, Malvern Hall, Warwickshire (1809).
National Gallery, London.

PLATE 35

a) CONSTABLE, The Hay Wain (*ca.* 1821).
Victoria and Albert Museum, London.

b) CONSTABLE, The Hay Wain (1821).
National Gallery, London.

PLATE 36

a) CONSTABLE, Salisbury Cathedral (*ca.* 1820).
National Gallery, London.

b) TURNER, Salisbury Cathedral (*ca.* 1828).
George Coats Collection, Glasgow.